Nevil Maskelyne

Modern Spiritualism

Nevil Maskelyne

Modern Spiritualism

ISBN/EAN: 9783742860385

Manufactured in Europe, USA, Canada, Australia, Japa

Cover: Foto ©Lupo / pixelio.de

Manufactured and distributed by brebook publishing software (www.brebook.com)

Nevil Maskelyne

Modern Spiritualism

MODERN SPIRITUALISM.

A SHORT ACCOUNT OF ITS RISE AND PROGRESS, WITH SOME EXPOSURES OF SO-CALLED SPIRIT MEDIA.

BY

JOHN NEVIL MASKELYNE,
ILLUSIONIST AND ANTI-SPIRITUALIST.

LONDON:
FOR THE AUTHOR BY
FREDERICK WARNE AND CO.,
BEDFORD STREET, STRAND.
New York: SCRIBNER, WELFORD, AND ARMSTRONG.

PREFACE.

I MUST claim the indulgence of the Public in thus venturing before them in a new character; but as I feel that great interest is taken in the question of "Spiritualism," I need offer no apology for the following pages.

In writing this I have no intention of hurting the feelings of the many amiable persons possessing this peculiar faith; but I shall not hesitate to ridicule the—to ordinary minds—absurd doctrines inculcated by their leaders, or to lay bare the miserable deceptions of the mediumistic craft.

I am convinced that many adherents of this so-called *religion* are "impressed" with the truth of the doctrines on very unsatisfactory grounds, that they are frequently in ignorance of its origin, and almost always of the goal to which it is tending. In this belief I have drawn facts from many sources (in all cases giving my authorities), to form a short account of the rise and progress of this "New Gospel;" of the wide divergence of opinion amongst "the faithful" as to what may or may not be accepted; of the credulity of its most distinguished followers; of the lives of its best-known leaders; and the exposures of many of its accredited agents, in which latter branch I may perhaps be allowed to speak with some authority, having succeeded in dethroning several of the *genus* "medium."

I have no desire to enter the lists with the scientific investigators of this greatest of modern delusions, and shall, therefore, steer as clear as possible of the *isms*,—merely mentioning such rocks ahead as "Psychic" or "Odic" Force, "Unconscious Cerebration," or other of the theories to account for "manifestations" which I hold to be altogether mundane in their origin, and mainly attributable to gross and harmful trickery and fraud.

The size of this little work precludes the idea of my treating the subject as a whole; I have, therefore, confined myself to a short History of the movement, and to a recital of the Exposures that have from time to time been made public.

It is my intention to produce a book—in continuation of this subject—which shall thoroughly expose and explain the tricks and *modus operandi* of the media, the Indian Fakirs (of whom Spiritualists talk so much), and other spirit jugglers.

Those who would go more deeply into the matter treated of in these pages than I have the time to write or the public the patience to read, may easily find plenty of Spiritualistic literature. They will certainly require nerve to go into it, and a strong brain to come out unscathed: for the public I trust this book may suffice to give an idea of the source and course of this "Pantheon of Progress," when, if they draw a little—just a little—moral at the conclusion I shall have gained my end.

Egyptian Hall, Piccadilly,
London.

CONTENTS.

CHAPTER I.
The old, old Love ... ... Page 1

CHAPTER II.
The Shakers' Lesson 12

CHAPTER III.
The Rochester Knockings 19

CHAPTER IV.
The Mystic Sensitive 31

CHAPTER V.
"Daniel" in the Lyon's Den 50

CHAPTER VI.
The Juggling Gemini 58

CHAPTER VII.
Our Spirit Guides 70

CHAPTER VIII.
The Mediumistic Craft 80

CHAPTER IX.
The Invasion of the Media 97

CHAPTER X.
A Few Exposures 115

CHAPTER XI.

Poor "John King!" 132

CHAPTER XII.

"Sweet Katey King!" 141

CHAPTER XIII.

Odds and Ends 154

CHAPTER XIV.

"The Pantheon of Progress" 178

CHAPTER I.

THE OLD, OLD LOVE.

Spiritualism—Light *Séances* in the Dark Ages—Old-fashioned Spirits—The Cock Lane Ghost—The Shaker Craze—New Ghosts for Old Ones—Science and the "Pantheon"—Spiritualism *v.* the Bible.

SPIRITUALISM, in one form or other, has ever plagued the world: it is "as old as the hills," and likely to last as long—being a natural product of weak minds; and, whether it speaks through the Delphic Oracle or a gin-drinking "medium," it is ever the same in its debasing effects upon the intellect.

In Britain we had a Spiritualism with the priesthood of the Druids, who held their mystic rites (*séances*) "within the circle of the *meini gwnyion* (white stones)," and we have had it ever since. Every variety of convulsive and cataleptic phenomena has been ascribed to it; every old house, with rats scampering behind its crumbling wainscots, has been haunted by the spirits of the departed; and ghostly forms have been conjured from the mists of evening, the spray of the waterfall, or, mayhap, the outline of some wandering "Jerusalem" earning his sparse meal upon the mountain-side. There is nothing in nature that has not been turned to account by lovers of the marvellous, by superstition, or—most potent cause—ignorance. We have had "sheeted ghosts" *ad nauseam:* Stockwell rejoiced in its plate-smashing sprite, and Tedwell in its demon drummer;—both the latter made some noise in the world, and all had believers in their day.

The Cock Lane ghost—a foreshadowing of some modern "physical manifestations"—was, *for a time*, a successful piece of trickery, even "taking in" the great lexicographer, Dr. Johnson, himself.

I must here diverge somewhat to give a sketch of this remarkable imposition for the benefit of the few unacquainted with its history.

Cock Lane—so called from the sign of the corner public house—was a narrow street running from Snow Hill to Smithfield. A man named Parsons lived here in 1754, and had, as lodgers, a Mr. and Mrs. Kempe. The latter dying, Parsons' daughter, aged eleven, whilst "possessed with the spirit" (which answered questions by "scratchings" or knocks—only heard when the girl medium was in bed) averred that the deceased lady had died from the effects of poison administered by her husband. A *post mortem* examination establishing the fact that Mrs. Kempe had died from natural causes, the "medium" and her accomplices were brought to trial before Lord Mansfield at the Guildhall, July 10th, 1756, when it was proved that the rapping sounds had been produced by a small piece of wood "used to stand the kettle on," which the sweetly innocent little treasure kept concealed within her stays. Being too young to be quite hardened, the precocious criminal confessed the fraud, adding that she had been instigated thereto by her father and mother. The sentence of the Court was that Parsons (who, it seems, owed money to Kempe, and had hit upon this new way to pay old debts) be imprisoned for two years, and stand three times in the pillory; his wife one year; and the dear little medium six months in Bridewell.

The Spiritualists of our day accept the kettle-stand taps as of spirit origin; indeed, it is difficult to find a ghost story in Mrs. Crowe's "Night Side of Nature" which does not add confirmation to those superstitious people who "swallow" Mr. Home's marvellous stories, and believe in intelligent communications from the parlour furniture. Now—

> "White-sheeted ghosts have grown mere fables;
> Instead of groaning, ghosts rap tables.
> *   *   *   *   *   *   *
> The grisly ghosts of old have vanished;
> The ancient bogies all are banished.
> How much more creditable and pleasant
> Than the old spirits are the present,"

says Mr. Punch, satirically. And surely there is a great falling off even in our superstitions!

> "The intelligible forms of ancient poets,
> The fair humanities of old religion,
> The power, the beauty, and the majesty
> That had their haunts in dale, or piny mountain,
> Or forest, or slow stream, or pebbly spring,
> Or chasms, or watery depths,—all these have vanished:
> They live no longer in the faith of reason."

The spirit that has moved the Quaker with "tremblings and twitchings" when the word of the Lord came to him has impelled the Shaker to dance, and, so they say, "impressed" the medium to tell lies.* The Quakers have become a very quiet sect now; and the Shakers make little noise in the world, save when, poor creatures! they are turned out of house and home; but the Spiritual-

---

* Mr. H. D. Jencken, a Spiritualist (husband to Kate Fox), considers that the great majority of spirit messages are "objectless lies."

ists are with us in full blast, with their peculiar faith, their strange "phenomena," and, stranger than all, their hybrid mediums, who act as a kind of a buffer between this and the next world. And what varied beliefs does this Spiritualism embrace! We have no two ideas alike as to mediums, the spirits, or the spirit world; and even the sect, if we can call it one, is doubtful of the "manifestations" among its own people. A committee of Spiritualists meeting at Cleveland, in 1867, reported that "What at present passes for spirit communion among the people is a mixed, and, for the most part, unanalysed mass, rendering the identity of spirit presence very uncertain. . . . Many, *if not all*, of the disorderly manifestations your committee deem wholly unspiritual, having their origin in half-controlled diseased nerves, poor digestion, torpid liver, and general discord of mind and body."

Was it "poor digestion and a torpid liver" that gave to Judge Edmonds his visions of the spheres with their strange spirits in the shape of monkeys, &c.? or does the "general discord of mind and body" cause Dr. Adin Ballou, one of the oldest and most distinguished Spiritualists in America, to affirm that intelligent answers can be received from the spirits of birds, beasts, and stones?

The few fanatics who would graft the "spirits"—and such spirits, too!—upon, or put them in place of, our simple faith, have made vigorous efforts to force upon the nineteenth century the stupid rapping delusion as a reality. Their "spirit guides," who lead to nothing good, their "controls," who require restraint, their miracles and their "gush," are all alike foreign to our English ideas. But, say you, there are Spiritualists here! Ay; a drop in an ocean! *The* PEOPLE *have never been touched.* The noxious weed which sprang up in America some thirty years back, and quickly overran that continent, though transplanted to our " tight little island," has never enjoyed the same lusty life as in its native soil. Doubtless, like all "spirits" in the past, the modern bogies will be laid ere long; and signs are not wanting that before another generation has passed away, not even the ghost of a follower of this modern form of the Spiritualistic craze will be discovered aboveground.

As I have said, it was reserved for Young America to perfect this latest phase of an old, old story. The affliction is a direct outcome of the teachings of that "prince of mystics," Emanuel Swedenborg, acting upon the impressionable minds of the Shakers of New Lebanon and Watervliet, N.Y. As if to prove that dullness has its ecstatics as well as genius, in the year 1843 these victims to the " new dispensation " " became the subjects of strange psychological experiences, during which certain of the members would lose all personal consciousness, while influences, purporting to be the spirits of persons of different nations, and who had lived in the world in different ages, took possession of their bodies, and spoke through their vocal organs."*

Our sharper American cousins soon afterwards turned all this to account, and have since manufactured professional media by the score, who have run the gipsies out of the field, predicting the future with equal truth (also "for a consideration"), and having the advantage of not being locked up for their nefarious practices.

Table-tilting, spirit-rapping, movements of the furniture, musical (!) performances, living persons "levited"—transported through the air—spirit writing, spirit faces, spirit lights, "materialized" hands, arms, and whole bodies, are amongst the tricks of the modern mediumistic trade; and

---

* "New American Cyclopædia." New York, 1863.

so far the fraudulent media have escaped punishment—if not the frauds detection—save in the photographic incident* at Paris.

Mesmerism, too, which in its "higher phenomena" has been rejected by the ablest scientific men, crops up again in the guise of Spiritualism, the *ecstasis* of to-day is the clairvoyance of yesterday, the only difference observable being that the Spiritualistic quackery is the more culpable of the two. Happily, I think, for us, science has demolished the entire superstructure of the "Pantheon," leaving in the universal wreck the table-turning phenomena † as attributable to a natural cause, some "animal magnetism," and such phenomena as come under the general head of nervous diseases.

Faraday—the "great master of experimental philosophy"—disposed of the supernatural origin of table-turning by the construction of a simple machine, which recorded the muscular movement of the persons forming the circle, and of which they were possibly unconscious.

Dr. Laycock's "Reflex Action of the Brain"—the foreshadowing of Sir William Hamilton's "Latent Thought"—and Dr. Carpenter's "Ideo-motor Principle," all pointed to what Faraday proved. Thus, in "unconscious cerebration," we have an easy solution of table-tilting, planchette, and similar phenomena, which have puzzled so many minds. Dr. Carpenter, lecturing at the Royal Institution, March 12th, 1852, said, "This ideo-motor principle finds its appropriate place in the physiological system, which would indeed be incomplete without it. And, when it is once recognized, it may be applied to the explanation of nume-

---

* See "Spirit Photos," Chapter X.

† Rapping, table-turning, &c., are declared by Spiritualists to be "only the fringe of the subject."

rous phenomena which have been a source of perplexity to many who have been convinced of their genuineness, and who could not see any mode of reconciling them with the known laws of nervous action. These phenomena have been clearly proved to depend upon the state of *expectant attention* on the part of the performer; his will being temporarily withdrawn from the control of his muscles by the state of abstraction to which his mind is given up, and the *anticipation* of a given result being the stimulus which directly and involuntarily prompts the muscular movements that produce it."

Another "scientist"—Von Reichenbach—has discovered in nature an Odic Force, or "nervous influence," to which he ascribes many of the phenomena of Spiritualism; but I am inclined to believe with Mr. Punch that they are mainly attributable to "That oldest of Od Force—folly!" Dr. Ashburner, in his translation of "Reichenbach's Researches," says: "There are organs of the brain which, when over-stimulated, leave the individual a victim of ecstacy. The imagination, said to be a mental faculty, but in reality the result of a combination of the actions of several organs, if indulged in without regulation and very strict control by the intellectual powers, may lead to an ecstacy as incompatible with rational conviction as the open-mouthed fatuous wonderment of the idiot is with the higher, calm reasoning power of the philosopher."

There is also the "Psychic Force" theory, broached by Serjeant Cox (much after Reichenbach's *Od* pattern), whereby "the medium, or the people associated together as a whole, is supposed to possess a force, power, influence, virtue, or gift, by means of which intelligent beings are enabled to produce the phenomena observed."*

---

* Before quitting the scientific theories, I should mention Mr Home's

Other scientific men have spoken out upon this question, some without propounding any theory to the elucidation of the impositions generally practised in the name of the spirits. Of these I may name Professors Tyndall and Huxley. The former denounces the belief as "degrading," and only acceptable to weak minds; the latter, in reply to a letter from the Dialectical Society requesting his co-operation in the investigation of the phenomena of Spiritualism, writes, under date January 29th, 1869: "The only case of Spiritualism I have had the opportunity of examining into for myself was as gross an imposture as ever came under my notice. . . . The only good that I can see in a demonstration of the truth of 'Spiritualism' is to furnish an additional argument against suicide. Better live a crossing sweeper than die and be made to talk twaddle by a 'medium' hired at a guinea a *séance*."

Dr. Carpenter, author of an article in the "Quarterly Review" on "Spiritualism and its recent Converts," (October, 1871), says: "We were requested to join a committee for investigating the supposed 'occult' powers possessed by the Davenport Brothers. Being informed that the members of the committee would be required, like ordinary attendants at the Brothers' performance, to join hands in a 'circle,' and that the essential part of the performances themselves took place either within a cupboard into which no one was permitted to look, or in a dark room, we replied that we did not consider these performances to be proper subjects of scientific inquiry, for that no scientific man could consent to forego the use of

---

story of the old woman in America who, being asked if she could account for what she had seen accomplished by the medium at a *séance*, replied, "Lor, sirs! it's easy enough: they only rubs theirselves all over with a gold pencil case!"

his eyes and his hands, the most valuable of all his instruments for the investigation of objective truth."

It comes to this: the tricks of modern Spiritualism as little stand investigation as they do the light of day. Its table-turning is turned from a supernatural to a natural cause; its trance-speaking is a sham; its rapping tables have not a leg left to stand upon; and to write the rapped-out rubbish as spirit communications is as false as the assertion that those aërial beings "revisit the glimpses of the moon" for the profit of disreputable "media."

But though science has done much to upset the Spiritual theory, we have not only the Spiritualists proper still clinging to it, but others who see in the manifestations only the work of the Father of Lies. In so doing, they give his Satanic Majesty much less credit for *nous* than he usually receives. Several clerical gentlemen have discovered that table-rapping is due to the influence of the Evil One: I may give an instance :—

COMMUNICATION RECEIVED BY RAPS.

"Are we justified by works?"—"Yes."
"By faith alone?"—"No."
"Is the whole Bible true?"—"No."
"Were the miracles of the New Testament wrought by supernatural power?"—"No."
"By some hidden law of nature?"—"Yes."

* * * *

"Is it right to pray to the Virgin?"—"Yes."
"Is Christ God?"—"No."
"Is He a man?"—"No."
"Is He something between God and man—a sort of angel?"—"Yes."

"Is He in heaven?"—"No."
"Where is He?"—It spelt slowly, "H, E, L, L."*

DIABLERIE *I* will none of!

If all the conflicting theories of Spiritualism itself were to be gathered together, each individual of that precious sect would be bewildered, and feel like Artemus Ward, who would "give five dollars to anybody that would tell him who he was and whar he was goin'!" Mr. William Howitt declares that its true mission is "to recall to the knowledge and restore to the consciousness of mankind the Christian faith, with all its divine and supernatural power," whilst the New Gospel itself was established by that "Seer of Poughkeepsie" who publicly scoffed at the Bible. The later apostles of Spiritualism, including Mr. Morse, I.O.G.T., have either a decided objection to the Divine Book, or accept it with a struggle, because—as they say—it teaches Spiritualism. At the first conference of the National Association of Spiritualists, held at Liverpool, August, 1873, Mr. J. Chapman, the Secretary, averred that "once he considered the Spiritual manifestations in the Bible to be ignorantly devised fables; but Spiritualism had since made him accept them as truth, and caused him to swallow not only Jonah, but the whale as well." † A Mr. Meredith was of opinion that if all the Spiritualism were to be taken out of the Bible, nothing would be left but the cover; and Mr. Morse, who as a medium reflects a brighter intellect than that of earth, desired his hearers to understand that "if the teachings of Spiritualism are in harmony with those of the Bible, well and good; if not, let them try to harmonize what teachings

---

* "Table-Turning." A Lecture by the Rev. R. W. Dibdin, M.A. London, 1853.

† The "Spiritualist" Newspaper, August 15th, 1873.

were useful and just, and put aside the rest." So that the Bible holds a very secondary position with these gentlemen, two of whom, at least, may fairly be claimed as representative men. Surely, Mr. Howitt, you must see that this is substituting something for Christianity, instead of "restoring it to the consciousness of mankind"! With the majority of your brethren the Bible is classed with works on demonology, witchcraft, animal magnetism, &c., &c., which all contain, to them, some corroboration of the truth of Spiritualism. Mr. Burns, Editor of the "Medium," declares, in that Spiritualistic sheet, which I shall have again and again to refer to, " an absolutely perfect medium, and, we may add, a successful truth-seeker, should be free from beliefs of all kinds. . . . Spiritualism comes to supplant all this nonsense with knowledge, or, in the absence of that, honest, healthy ignorance, which is indeed a condition of the appetite for truth"!*

I may leave Messrs. Howitt and Burns to settle these little differences of opinion as they can, and proceed to sketch the lives of a few prominent men and women in the movement, to tabulate the impositions of the media, and note the gullibility of the faithful. We shall make the acquaintance of such of the latter as are most familiar with the spirit land and its occupants; in company with the medial gentry we shall learn something of the phenomenal formation of the spirit face and the materialized spirit form; and we shall be introduced behind the scenes, where the media are taking off the spirit masks, folding up the spirit dresses (the fabric hailing from Manchester), dividing the proceeds of the last "show," and preparing for the next.

---

* "Medium and Daybreak," September 17th, 1875.

CHAPTER II.

THE SHAKERS' LESSON.

The Poughkeepsie Seer—Birth, Parentage, and Education—A "pleasing mystical circumstance"—"Stumping the Provinces"—The *Principles of Nature*—Trance Poetry—Visits to the Spheres—Predictions—The "New Gospel" started.

ANDREW JACKSON DAVIS, also known as "the Seer of Poughkeepsie," is perhaps the most remarkable man in the history of modern Spiritualism, of which he was the pioneer; "the first of that innumerable company of Spiritualists, which, like a flood, has since inundated every State in America north and south of Dixie's Land."

He was born at Blooming Grove, Orange Co., N.Y., August 11th, 1826, and his parents being extremely poor, he is said to have been left in a state of complete ignorance. Sent at an early age to tend cattle, he was so stupid that his brothers and sisters made a laughingstock of him, and his father declared "he would never earn his salt, for he had not gumption enough to make a whistle." Andy, however, soon showed more ability than his father's remark would warrant, as his communications with the "higher intelligences" began shortly afterwards. Of this turning-point in his life he gives the following account in his autobiography, "The Magic Staff":

"Being allowed the freedom of the house, my master's children would frequently unite with and aid me in trying to sing Washingtonian Temperance Songs. One Sunday while singing

"'Where are the friends that to me were so dear,
Long, long ago,' &c.,

there happened a pleasing mystical circumstance, of which I was the sole recipient. When we sang the words

"'In their graves laid low,'

I heard the word *no!* distinctly and emphatically shouted in my ear.

"'Don't do that, Russel,' said I to the eldest son.

"'Do what?' he inquired, with a look of surprise.

"'Don't holler *no!* when 'taint in the song,' I pleadingly exclaimed.

"'I didn't,' he quickly replied. 'I didn't hear it neither.'

"The younger children, Austin and Freddy, also denied any participation. So we proceeded with our singing; but whenever we sang the affirmative that our friends are

"'In their graves laid low,'

I would hear the negative *no!* as clear and positive as any word pronounced by ourselves. At the time I could not comprehend it."

About the year of the Shaker craze, Davis *père* removed to Poughkeepsie, and "young hopeful," the unsophisticated child of nature, was "taken in hand by one Levingston, the village tailor, and found possessed of remarkable powers of clairvoyance." He began to converse freely upon medical and psychological subjects while in a state of magnetic trance, and subsequently he commenced the treatment of disease. "He soon informed his magnetizer that the great object of his powers was to enable him to examine and prescribe for the sick. There was no disputing such a prudent and charitable impression as this. Mr. Levingston, as a matter of course, immediately perceived and acknowledged the full purport of it; and both he and his *protégé* agreed, the one to abandon his goose, and the other his last" (he had joined his father in the cobbling business), "and take to what in American parlance is called 'stumping the provinces.'" *

Thus about his twentieth year, Davis quitted Poughkeepsie. He soon turned his back upon his father and poor Levingston, joining Dr. Silas Smith and the Rev. William Fishbough, both of whom with Yankee 'cuteness saw money in the youth if properly "worked." Under the new management he rapidly acquired higher powers—entering into what he terms a state of "clairscience," but which his former "guide, philosopher, and friend," the ex-village tailor, denounced as humbug—the bold Levingston actually accusing Lyon the Fourierist, and Fishbough the Universalist, of being joint authors of the young clairvoyant's "inspired" works. Truth to say, when his amanuensis (Fishbough) and Dr. Lyon leave him, he cuts but a sorry figure in that line! Under the wing of Fishbough the youthful "seer," *whilst in a trance state*, dictated a work, entitled "The Principles of Nature: Her Divine Revelations, and a Voice to Mankind," and straightway was dubbed—"The Guide and Leader of the Age." His *Principles* is "a chaos of unarranged matter," treating of "cosmogany, astronomy, geology, ethnology, archæology, mythology, theology, psychology, history, metaphysics,

---

* "Edinburgh Review."

&c.," besides "soaring flights of mind into regions not previously explored by any human being; or revelations of strange spheres, as well as their stranger economies—the existence of which was never suspected by the most inquisitive nor conceived by the most whimsical of mortals in this or any other age." " Excepting so far as relates to the regions not previously explored by any earthly being," says the "Edinburgh Review," "the book has no claim whatever to the character of originality. Its facts and its fictions, its creeds and its theories—all alike have been systematically plagiarized, and gravely reproduced oftentimes, with barely a verbal disguise, as the authentic teachings of disembodied spirits, and of higher intelligences 'impressed' upon the sensorium of an illiterate cowherd. It is a mad jumble of Spinozism, Fourierism, St. Simonianism, Swedenborgianism, and Rationalism. Davis—or rather his unscrupulous guardians (for that docile youth was as yet unequal to the task ascribed to him)—have laid under tribute every pantheistic and infidel writer, from the age of Bruno to that of Strauss, in order to build up their own monstrously paradoxical scheme of Spiritomaterialism."

But we will let Davis or his mentors speak in one or two extracts from the "Principles": "In the BEGINNING the Univercœlum was one boundless, indefinable, and unimaginable ocean of LIQUID FIRE! The most vigorous and ambitious imagination is not capable of forming an adequate conception of the height, and depth, and length, and breadth thereof." Man, according to this brilliant work, was originally "an oyster or clam," which produced a tadpole; the tadpole a quadruped; the quadruped a baboon; the baboon an orang-outang; the orang-outang a negro; and the negro a white man. "The original inhabitants of the earth were black, the subsequent nations were brown ; the branches of these were red ; from these spread the yellow, and from these the white." *

Davis's Theology is "written on the widespread scroll of the heavens, in which every star is a word, and every constellation a sentence ;" his philosophy is ultra-material, for "all things, whether tangible or intangible, are material . . . I use the terms 'spiritual,' 'celestial,' or 'heavenly,' as representing distinct degrees of material refinement."

The universe is divided by Davis into seven spheres and forty-nine circles, in the centre of which is our earth ; he has a vision of the creation of this "rudimentary sphere," and gives it in the following rudimentary verse. Let us hope he is not the nearest approach to a Milton the Great Republic possesses.

> "My spirit grew up and seemed to expand
> Beyond books of men, and creeds of the land.
> A wild terrific grandeur spread around,
> Seas of lava gurgled up from depths profound ;
> Lightnings waltzed with lightnings o'er the sea ;
> Thunders vied with thunders in frantic glee ;
> Motion was married to motion with one consent,
> And atom wedded atom with one intent.
> Motion and atoms in nuptial pairs appeared,
> And Method was to Matter more endeared.
> But swiftly rolled the blazing orb along,
> Less eccentric daily—more sedate and strong.
> Its fierce fiery face was cooled by the air ;
> Passion had less reign—the scene grew more fair.
> Among the stars, 'twas decided by a vote
> That young Earth should wear a granite coat ;
> But, heaving with hidden fires, and angry yet,
> He fretted and frowned like a demon's pet ;
> Still his face seemed cold, and bare, and grand,
> But water quickly formed, and covered all the land ;
> A bath so cold soon chilled the fiery swain,
> And, quaking at the centre, he burst in twain !

---

* "Principles of Nature," page 366.

> Earth's coat, though granite, was 'tattered and torn,
> And his face, tho' rough, was 'shaven and shorn;'
> But like the wound which God the devil gave,
> The opening closed, yet left an open grave:
> In plunged the waters from the vast profound,
> And here and there exposed a little ground.
> He bellowed and quaked, and clanked his chain,
> And vomited forth both mounts and main.
> I saw hills on hills, Alps on Alps arise,
> And a marriage betwixt all seas and skies.
> A carbonic air, encircling all the main,
> Shut out the spangled skies from peak to plain:
> The world-wide storm swelled the sea-lord's breast,
> And the thunderbolt forger felt all the rest.
> Old Neptune's trident shook both land and sea,
> And Vulcan telegraphed Venus down to tea." *

In the spheres—" the Summer Land "—which surround this "rudimentary earth," the spirit emancipated from the body has all the enjoyments of this world without its care or sorrow. The spirits have their spheres allotted to them according to intellectual or moral status, and are continually advancing towards the Seventh, which, when reached, all are upon an equality.

The "Seer," notwithstanding his personal visits to the planets Saturn, Jupiter, Mars, Venus, and Mercury, found time to run through a portion of the States, delivering lectures and inaugurating the new movement.

In addition to the numerous voluminous works published in his name, he also undertook the editorship of the "Banner of Light," an American periodical (Boston) devoted to Spiritualism; and, as a publisher, he scattered broadcast over the English-speaking world a flood of the peculiar literature so dear to " the faithful few," and so unreadable and unremunerative to the general public.

In the autumn of 1846, Davis had predicted that "*ere*

---

* The "Great Harmonia," Vol. V., page 366.

long the communication with the spirit world would take the form of a living demonstration." Upon this hint the rapping spake ! and in 1848, while all America was lost in wonder at the mystic flights of the Poughkeepsie " Seer," his teachings first bore fruit in the physical manifestations of the Fox and Fish families in the now famous "Rochester knockings."

So the " New Gospel" was started by a 'cute Yankee, whose "ecstatic" dreams have been turned to golden realities by his followers—some of whom appear to have discovered that philosopher's stone which Dr. Dee* so panted for and failed to find.

Is it not strange that Spiritualism, whose true mission is to restore the Christian faith "to the consciousness of mankind," should owe so much to a materialist who scoffed at the Bible and denied the existence of sin?

---

* Dr. Dee was an early professor of spiritual legerdemain, and called his spirits into that innocent-looking black stone—or, as Butler calls it, "The Devil's Looking-glass,"—now to be seen at the Alexandra Palace. His *Magical Speculum* (No. 1,290 in the Londesborough Collection) is a circular black stone with a highly polished surface ; it is flat, and about half an inch thick by seven and a half inches in diameter. In the same collection may be seen the crystal balls used by sorcerers in the sixteenth century, in which they were supposed to produce the visions of the absent or departed for their dupes.

On looking at the " Medium and Daybreak " for December 10th, 1875, I find we still have a "crystal seer" with us in London.

CHAPTER III.

THE ROCHESTER KNOCKINGS.

The Corner Stone of the "Pantheon"—American Rapper-ees—Lively Bed-"ticking"—"Old Splitfoot"—"Murder will out"—*Grave* doubts—Profitable Spirits—Rapid *resumé* of Rapping Theories—A queer *Fish*—Mediumistic Babies.

DAVIS having cleared the ground and uprooted all the old beliefs, the building of the "Pantheon" commenced.

Not with a flourish of trumpets nor by dignitaries of the land, but in a very humble wooden dwelling-house in an obscure Yankee village, the corner stone of the edifice was laid by two little girls.

Our story proper, then, opens about the year 1847, at Hydesville, Arcadia, Rochester County, N.Y., with something like a postman's rap upon the door of one Mr. Michael Weekman.* The rapping continuing, this gentleman, being unable to trace it to any visible cause, did

---

* The sounds were said to have been first heard in this house by Mrs. Ann and Miss Lucretia Pulver, in 1844; but as their account was given *after* the "mysterious knockings" of the Foxes had gained notoriety, I may be excused for doubting the veracity of the gentle Pulvers.

what many another weak man would have done under the same circumstances,—he vacated the premises. Mr. John D. Fox and his family thereupon entered into possession in December, 1847, and early in the following year they were "startled" by mysterious rappings in many parts of the house, and all "helped search"—as Mrs. Fox says—for the cause. These noises increased "in loudness and frequency" up to the end of March, and not the slightest clue to their origin could be discovered. The spirits were coy; but it was not to last long. When they did begin, like a Welsh river in a flood, they broke all bounds. The evening of the last day of March came, and as the family had been disturbed for many previous nights by the rapping, they retired early. Mrs. Fox had seen her two youngest children — Margaret, aged twelve years, and Kate, nine—nicely tucked in between the sheets, when the sounds were again heard. Mrs. Fox says: "My husband had not gone to bed when we first heard the noise on this evening; I had just lain down. It commenced as usual. I knew it from all other sounds I had ever heard in the house. The girls who slept in the other bed in the room heard the noise, and tried to make a similar noise by snapping their fingers." Such peculiar bed-ticking might naturally be supposed to alarm the Fox children, who might then have been called Fox's martyrs; but the contrary seems to have been the case. I think it was Mr. Henry Russell who sang, in his capital Entertainment, some years ago—

> "You little know what great things
> From little things may rise,"

and surely that sly little Fox—Katey—could scarcely have realized the gravity of the occasion when she began imitating the raps! For, "being a lively child, and in a measure accustomed to what was going on, she turned to where the noise was, snapped her fingers, and called out 'Here, old Splitfoot, do as I do,'" (which was shocking for a little lady of nine) "and *the knocking instantly responded.*"*

Mamma Fox, who must have had an intuitive idea that the spirits were at the bottom of it all, said to the unknown rapper, " Count ten," and was instantly obeyed. " Fifteen " was called for with a like result, and then Mrs. Fox said, " Tell us the age of Cathy" (the youngest daughter—our sly little Kate!) " by rapping one for each year," and Miss Katey received her proper number of years in distinct raps, which, being such a young lady, she could afford to do. Then Mrs. Fox, coming straight to the point, said," If you are a spirit, rap twice," and she received two particularly affirmative raps.

" This was the very commencement," says Robert Dale Owen; "who can tell where the end will be?" Who, indeed, poor Owen! The rumour of these disturbances quickly spread in that little community, and neighbours— the Redfields, the Dueslers, the Hydes, and the Jewells— all came from their wooden shanties, eager to gossip, and open to the marvellous, as ignorance always is.

Soon the news travelled, and persons from a distance flocked in until the excitement became intense. The rapping, too, began to assume coherency, and was soon giving the details of a murder which had been committed in the house occupied by this (very) " Foxy" family. Thus the first spirit, in the modern phase of the "ism," was that of a pedlar, who declared—through the table-legs—that he had been knocked off *his* " pins" (*i.e.*, murdered) by a former occupant of the premises, a certain John C. Bell, a

---

* " Footfalls on the Boundary of another World." R. D. Owen.

blacksmith; and the spirit-pedlar further informed his gaping audience that his trunk was packed up, and all the members of his body neatly disposed of beneath some ten feet of earth in the cellar. Now, it is said to be beyond doubt that some portion of a skeleton was found at the precise spot indicated; but it is also said that opinion was more than equally divided in favour of its being, not the framework of humanity, but the well-picked bones of a sheep! "A man named Bell did come from a distant part of the country, and attempted to exculpate himself by swearing that he knew nothing about it. For want of *legal* evidence, no steps could, of course, be taken against the accused, and so far as he was concerned the matter dropped."* As Mr. Bell does not seem to have been well read up in the Cock Lane ghost story, he did not prosecute the Foxes, or they might have been "run to earth," much as dear little medium Parsons was some years before. Notwithstanding that no sepulchral knell was straightway rung for this "dreadful Bell," the *manes* of the defunct pedlar (or sheep) seem to have been satisfied, for the bones never rattled again. Indeed, some even doubted if any bones were found at all, and declared that the missing pedlar afterwards re-appeared at Hydesville, "still 'clothed with mortality,' and having a new assortment of wares to sell." † However this may be, the rapping continued. It was becoming a paying thing, for multitudes now flocked from all parts to inquire into the phenomena, to the no small profit of the Fox family. Soon after this the girls were removed to Rochester, a town on the borders of Lake Ontario, where they resided with Mrs. Fish, a married sister, a teacher of music, who now rapidly developed into a medium, and arranged a code of signals, in which the old system of

---

* "Where are the Dead?".   † "Humbugs of the World."

receiving one rap as a negative, two as doubtful, and three as an affirmative, was supplanted by calling over the alphabet, the "spirits" rapping at the required letter, and so spelling the message out, in very bad orthography. Five raps, included in the code, was a signal that the alphabet was required.

In November, 1849, so great was the excitement that a meeting was held in the Corinthian Hall, Rochester, to inquire into the phenomena, at which the Committee of Investigation gave the subject up in despair. Deluded creatures! Had they only known that *rubbing the sole or upper part of the shoe against the polished legs of a table would produce the rapping sounds!* That they can be so obtained is a fact; and who shall say that those little mice-like feet peeping out beneath the skirts of Margaret and Katey Fox, may not have operated upon the mahogany four-poster and the loo-table (if they had such in their humble dwelling), to produce the phenomena?* But there are many ways of obtaining raps without the "kettle-stand" or boots upon well-polished mahogany. I have produced them regularly before my audience by a simple trick; and Dr. Schiff has propounded a theory, according to which "the repeated displacement of the tendon of the *peroneus longus* muscle in the sheath in which it slides behind the external *malleolus*" will produce the sounds.†

---

* These precocious children remind us of the "Edinburgh Review"(1854) notice of Joe Smith, the Vermont boy:—"Children are flattered by the notice which they excite by such pretensions; and, if the credulity of their elders gives them encouragement, are easily tempted to go on from lie to lie. For there is, perhaps, no period of life more sensible than childhood to the delights of notoriety."

† "John King" says the spirits have two ways of producing raps; but he only describes one, which is above ordinary comprehension. The spirits, he says,

Mrs. Norman Culver, of Arcadia, made a deposition, upon April 17th, 1871, to the effect that one of the girls had instructed her how to produce the raps with her toe-joints; and Mrs. Culver actually produced similar sounds in the presence of a magistrate and others. The following is the text of

MRS. CULVER'S STATEMENT.

"I am, by marriage, a connection of the Fox girls. Their brother married my husband's sister. The girls have been a great deal at my house; and for about two years I was a very sincere believer in the rappings; but something which I saw when I was visiting the girls at Rochester, made me suspect that they were deceiving. I resolved to satisfy myself in some way; and some time afterwards I made a proposition to Catherine to assist her in producing the manifestations. I had a cousin visiting me from Michigan, who was going to consult the spirit, and I told Catherine that if they intended going to Detroit, it would be a great thing for them to convince him. I also told her that if I could do anything to help her, I would do it cheerfully; that I should probably be able to answer all the questions he would ask, and I would do it if she would show me how to make the raps. She said that as Margaretta was absent, she wanted somebody to help her, and that if I would become a medium, she would explain it all to me. She said that when my cousin consulted the spirits, I must sit next to her, and touch her arm when the right letter was called. I did so, and was able to answer nearly all the questions correctly. After I had helped her in this way a few times,

---

gather the *aura* surrounding the medium, mould it in their hands, and throw it upon the table, &c., where it makes an explosive sound.

she revealed to me the secret. The raps are produced by the toes. All the toes are used. After nearly a week's practice with Catherine showing me how, I could produce them perfectly myself.

"At first it was very hard work to do it. Catherine told me to warm my feet, or put them in warm water, and it would then be easier work to rap. She said that she sometimes had to warm her feet three or four times during the course of an evening. I found that heating my feet did enable me to rap a great deal easier. I have sometimes produced a hundred and fifty raps in succession. I can rap with all the toes on both feet: it is most difficult to rap with the great toe. Catherine told me how to manage to answer the questions. She said it was generally easy enough to answer right, if the one who asked the questions called the alphabet. She said the reason why she asked people to write down several names on paper, and then point to them till the spirit rapped at the right one, was to give them a chance to watch the countenance and motions of the person, and that in that way they could nearly always guess right. She also explained how they held down and moved tables. (Mrs. Culver here gave some illustrations of the tricks.) She told me that all I should have to do to make raps heard on the table, would be to put my foot on the bottom of the table when I rapped, and that when I wished to make the raps sound distant on the wall, I must make them louder, and direct my own eyes earnestly to the spot where I wished them to be heard. She said if I could put my foot to the bottom of the door, the raps would be heard on the top of the door.

"Catherine told me that when her feet were held down by the Rochester Committee, the Dutch servant-girl rapped with her knuckles under the floor from the cellar. The girl was instructed to rap whenever she heard their voices calling the spirits. Catherine also showed me how they made the sounds of sawing and planing boards. When I was at Rochester last January, Margaretta told me that when people insisted on seeing her feet and toes, she could produce a few raps with her knees and ankles.

"Elizabeth Fish (Mrs. Fish's daughter), who now lives with her father, was the first one who produced these raps. She accidentally discovered the way of making them by playing with her toes against the foot-board while in bed. Catherine told me that the reason why Elizabeth went West to live with her father, was because she was too conscientious to become a medium. The whole secret was revealed to me, with the understanding that I should practise as a medium when the girls were away. Catherine said that whenever I practised, I had better have my little girl with me, and make folks believe that she was the medium; 'for,' she said, 'they would never suspect so young a child of any tricks.' After I had obtained the entire secret, I plainly told Catherine that my only object was to find out how these tricks were done, and that I should never go any further in this imposition. She was very much frightened, and said she believed I meant to tell of it and expose them; and if I did, she would swear it was a lie. She was so nervous and excited that I had to sleep with her that night. When she was instructing me how to be a medium, she told me how frightened they used to get in New York, for fear somebody would detect them, and gave me the whole history of all the tricks they played upon the people there. She said that once Margaretta spoke aloud, and that the whole party believed it was a spirit.

(Signed), "MRS. NORMAN CULVER."

CERTIFICATE.

"We hereby certify that Mrs. Culver is one of the most respectable and intelligent ladies in the town of Arcadia. We were present when she made the disclosures. We had heard the same from her before, and we cheerfully bear testimony that there cannot be the slightest doubt of the truth of the whole statement.

(Signed), "C. J. POMEROY, M.D.
"Rev. D. S. CHASE."

I note it as a significant fact that Spiritualist writers ignore Mrs. Culver's testimony altogether. From my own personal experience, I can fully endorse the foregoing statement.

By the time the Fox girls reached New York city in May, 1850, they were the talk of all America; and though their time was much occupied, it was not unprofitably so, as they are said to have done a "big thing"—in American parlance—by it, taking no less than five hundred thousand dollars from the credulous crowds flocking to witness, or hear, their spiritual wonders! True it is that the rapping was tedious; that, on the face of it, the communication was a clumsy one *for the spirits;* and that the Professors of the Medical College of Buffalo had thrown grave doubts over the *bonâ fides* of the affair, reporting that these loosely-constructed girls got their "raps" by snapping their toe and knee-joints;—yet, withal, the golden stream poured in!

Mrs. Fish seems to have been a medium with an eye to the main chance, but occasionally indiscreet. The spirit who "directed" a gentleman to take the medium down to the saloon "to get some oysters," seems to be of a very mundane origin; but when one of Mrs. Fish's familiars from the upper spheres declared that "the spirits live on pork and beans" in those elevated regions, we are put to the painful alternative of either doubting the veracity of a lady or the truthfulness of a spirit.

However, such little drawbacks notwithstanding, the success of the Fox girls, as well as that of their sister, was unbounded, and soon produced shoals of imitators, for, presently, every rap-scallion in the country was setting up as a medium. They are an ingenious race, those Yankees, and they understand business. The rapping paid, but something new must be forthcoming to keep up the excitement, so table-turning and tilting was discovered and ascribed to spiritual agency. At this, New York State went mad; Massachusetts followed suit; and before long our American cousins, from Maine to California, were running wildly after tables and chairs.

The ball was thus fairly set rolling; like one of snow, it has grown in its progress, and like that it will dissolve. Little by little new phenomena have been added, until not only tables are raised, but the spirits of the departed "in their habits as they lived." It is the "Pantheon of Progress," and its priests—the media—can perform miracles, even to the curing of disease by the simple laying on of hands; it is a New Gospel, the daybreak of a happier era for humanity. Oh, wondrous Yankee Doodle! inventor of wooden nutmegs and new religions, how you can be Barnumized! The Foxes have retired somewhat into the background now, and there are "new lights" in the mediumistic firmament, but little Katey Fox will ever be known as the real founder of the physical manifestations of modern Spiritualism. Now, she is Katey Fox no longer! On the 14th of December, 1872, Henry Diedrich Jencken, barrister-at-law, took the lady to be his wife at Marylebone Church, London, and there are now two little Jenckens, who inherit the medial properties of their mamma. The eldest, "Ferdy" (Ferdinand Leowenstein, aged two years), "when only five months old, wrote long messages in a clear handwriting;* he was carried from one room to another by an unseen being; and he was rocked in his cradle and attended by spirit forms."

"In his own home," says the "Spiritualist,"† "the medium boy is, as might be expected, only the baby boy; but every now and again the wondrous powers of this strangely-endowed child manifest themselves; his luminous eyes, as once described by his father in these pages, brighten into quite a lustre of soft light; he will stretch out his hands to catch his playmates—the unseen—whom he greets with smiles and caresses. Frequently the spirits will take his little foot, as they years ago used to do with little Kate Fox, and make it stamp on the floor or knock against the table, or they will move his tiny hand. At first this mode of communication was not understood; but on questions being put, the presence of an intelligent spiritual being was proven beyond doubt. To make certain, his mother requested that he should be made to rap seven, then five times, or answer questions. In reply to questions not addressed to him, but spoken in a low tone, which of course the little two-year-old could not understand, he then with his foot would rap out answers. The fact that his hand and foot were moved by spiritual beings was further proved by the dear little fellow showing his ankle, and saying, 'There, there! Hurt, hurt!' pointing to the spot where a spirit-hand had grasped him. Instances of the power of this child could be multiplied; but enough has been said to all but justify a belief that part of the pro-

---

* No. 214 of the "Medium and Daybreak" contains facsimiles of this.
† August 6th, 1875.

phecy given out by the spiritual beings in the winter of 1869 may be realized. We quote from Epes Sargent, treating on 'The Proof Palpable of Immortality.' In alluding to Kate Fox—her reliability, her powers, and her child—he cites a prophecy concerning her boy which was given at the house of Mr. H. P. Townsend six years ago : ' Kate will be married and will have a child who will be the wonder of the world. Kate will be a cypher in comparison ; she will only be remembered as his mother.' '*His* mother?' said Mrs. Townsend ; 'it is to be a boy!'"

So I leave Kate Fox Jencken and her little boys. No one can have the slightest objection to the father and mother thinking their little cherubs wonders—as, indeed, all children are !—but I trust we may be spared the multiplication of that threatened scourge—the Mediumistic Baby !

CHAPTER IV.

THE MYSTIC SENSITIVE.

An infant Daniel—" Furniture removed at the shortest notice "—" Daniel" visits England—A fig for the Scientists—" Daniel" takes his walks *abroad*— Bed-chamber Manifestations— Marriage — " How to make *Home* happy "—The shining light snuffed out at Rome—Pen-and-ink Sketches of " Daniel "—Elongation—" Airy Daniel "—" Sludge the Medium."

THE foundations of the "Pantheon" being in, the raising of the edifice seems to have been greatly entrusted to the "Mystic Sensitive," Daniel Dunglass Home.

The infant Daniel was of a delicate and nervous temperament, and if his aunt, who adopted him when he was about twelve months old, is to be credited with speaking the truth, he was the special object of attention from the spirits, his cradle being frequently rocked as if by guardian angels ! When nine years of age he accompanied his aunt and her husband to America, and delicate and nervous temperaments being rather at a premium there, he soon attained to considerable notoriety when the " Rochester knockings " broke out. Some startling " manifestations " created quite a storm in a tea-cup at home, where his aunt resented the bad habits of the "spirits" in knocking her furniture about. But Home, who is quite a modern Munchausen, shall tell a story anent this business—he was now seventeen years of age, and already an adept at "throwing the hatchet."

"When sitting quietly in the room with my aunt and uncle, the table, and sometimes the chairs and other furniture, were moved about in a singular way, to the great disgust and surprise of my relations. Upon one occasion, as the table was being moved about of itself, my aunt brought the family Bible, and placing it upon the table, said, 'There, that will soon drive the devils away;' but to her astonishment, the table only moved in a more lively manner, as if pleased to bear such a burden. Seeing this, she was greatly incensed, and determining to stop it, she angrily placed her whole weight on the table, and was actually lifted up with it bodily from the floor."*

No wonder, after this, that he should go into the spirit line of business, of which he has since been so distinguished an ornament! But, unlike your vulgar media, Home never received payment. How he obtained a livelihood, or what "presents" he received, we are not told.

"In 1852," he says, "frequently I had *séances* six or seven times a day, at each of which as many were present as could be accommodated. The house was besieged by visitors, and often outside in the street there was a concourse of anxious inquirers." He also increased the wonder of his performances, for, not content with moving a table (without castors) upon which five men, "whose united weight was *eight hundred and fifty-five pounds*," "from four to eight inches" (this is scarcely sufficiently explicit), he "conducts" other "experiments," which, as they are mainly

---

* "Incidents of my Life." D. D. Home. London 1863.

vouched for by this modern Cagliostro* himself, I need not further indicate here.

Having succeeded in putting blinkers on those high-metalled Yankees, who are so " tarnation 'cute" as to pride themselves upon being able " to see through a millstone," Home " fixed his young affections on " John Bull, as the next to be taken in and done for ; so, in March, 1855, he started for England. A concourse of fortuitous circumstances crowding together soon after his arrival in London, placed Home in a position which neither by ability nor zeal could he have occupied. He came to England early in the movement; he had energy from his Scotch extraction, and the indigenous impudence of his almost native land of Bunkum; he produced here tricks which had never been seen on this side of the Atlantic, though they were said to be common enough in America; and his great feat of " levitation "—or floating in the air—was copied from that performed by Henry Gordon, who "slid upstairs upon the banister of the stair-way, and then turned and *slid down head foremost* in the same manner, all by an invisible power." † There are other persons who profess to be able to " swim " in the air, and Spiritualism has as much to do with such trickery as it has with the Transit of Venus. So Home, skilful in the arts of elongation ‡ and contraction, of handling red-hot coals (*à la* the Fire King at Cremorne), and lighting gas with his finger-tips; used to being " chaired " (like the successful candidate at a good old-fashioned election) by the spirits, and to making mahogany frisk and accordions play without touch of hands; able to

---

* Though Home is a long way behind that great master of alchemy and astrology, Guiseppe Balsamo, of Palermo, *alias* Count Cagliostro.

† "Cridge's Epitome of Spiritual Intercourse."

‡ Elongation is quite a common thing now amongst the media. Indeed, there is enough of it to suggest a "*Long* firm" in the mystic fraternity !

call spirits from the vasty deep, and to work miracles of healing by their aid—though always posing *himself* as an interesting invalid—this high-priest of the order, and most fluent retailer of the jargon of modern Spiritualism, was soon the talk of London.

He was twenty-two years of age. Dr. J. J. G. Wilkinson* says: "the marks of consumption were legible upon his frame," and that he was "a modest, intelligent youth." The intelligence may be granted; the other statements are less reliable, I fancy. Twenty years have passed away since then, and Home, still "delicate" (though Dr. Mack's influence upon him was "simply magical") is alive, so the consumption cannot be a galloping one. He was in London in September, 1875, with "Mr. Aksakof, of St. Petersburg," looking after a new edition of his first volume of Apocrypha; for Daniel—canny Scot!—has ever an eye to the "siller"! I am sorry I did not see the great one during this visit, that I might say how time's ravages have dealt with him. You can see his portrait, by H. W. Pickersgill, R.A., painted about 1863, at the premises of the National Association of Spiritualists, or a later one in the "Medium" of January 7th, 1876; and you shall have the advantage of one or two pen-and-ink sketches of the distinguished "Seer." His appearance soon after he came to England (1855) is thus described by a writer in the now defunct "Morning Star": he was "thin and lithe," with "dainty white fingers and the neatest of wristbands." He wore a quantity of jewellery, including a monstre locket, and a diamond ring sparkled upon one of the fingers of his left hand. As for being "modest," many a one with

---

* Who is gifted with strong imaginative powers, for when Home plays upon an accordion he avers that he "never heard silence *threaded with such silver lines*"!

less nerve than this vain, self-confident man, with the sharp eyes that missed nothing, has floated a bubble company. Home found levitation much safer and more profitable. His first haven of rest was Cox's Hotel, Jermyn Street, St. James's. Here, he says, " In less than a month I had more engagements than I could well fulfil." Amongst his many visitors were Lord Brougham and Sir David Brewster. They stayed for a *séance*, the late Mr. William Cox, with the " mystic sensitive," being also present. In consequence of some exaggerated stories being circulated as to what took place upon this occasion, Sir David wrote a letter to the " Morning Advertiser," which was silently acquiesced in by Lord Brougham. It was dated " Carnock House, September 29th, 1855," and proceeds to say : " Were Mr. Home to assume the character of Wizard of the West, I would enjoy his exhibition as much as that of other conjurors; but when he pretends to possess the power of introducing among the feet of his audience the spirits of the dead, bringing them into physical communication with their dearest relatives, and of revealing the secrets of the grave, he insults religion and common sense, and tampers with the most sacred feelings of his victims."

In a subsequent letter Sir David wrote :

" 1. It is not true that a large dinner-table was moved about at Mr. Cox's in the most extraordinary manner.

" 2. It is not true that a large accordion was conveyed by an invisible or any other agency into my hand. I took it up myself, and it would not utter a sound.

" 3. It is not true that the accordion was conveyed into Lord Brougham's hand. It was placed in it.

"4. It is not true that the accordion *played an air throughout* in Lord Brougham's hands : it merely squeaked."

For this telling the truth, Sir David found himself

violently attacked in the papers by friends of the "mystic" one. They abused him as if he had been a pickpocket — as, indeed, they will me when they read this book, but I am pretty well used to their denunciations.

The controversy raised by these attacks upon Sir David was of the greatest benefit to Home, who was thus brought prominently before the public.

It is a noteworthy fact that up to this time all, or nearly all, the effects were produced *under a table*—the place afterwards chosen by Mr. Crookes for his wonderful accordion test; but as believers came about him, Home dropped this tentative style of doing things, and is said to have performed astounding feats before them. After leaving Cox's Hotel, Home retired to Ealing, and in the autumn of 1855 he repaired to Florence — the "manifestations" getting him into the best society. Here he remembers "upon one occasion, while the Countess C—— was seated at one of Erard's grand action pianos, it rose and balanced itself in the air during the whole time she was playing."

But this "trick" has been "trumped" by a Mrs. Young, of Twenty-Seventh Street, New York, who makes *her* piano answer questions, and stand upon an egg without crushing the shell ! *

An English lady resident at Florence in a haunted house, had Home up to exorcise the ghost. They sat at a table and received a communication by the spirit alphabet from the evil genius of the house ; then, the lady says in her narrative, " Mr. Home proposed that we should move into the next room—my bed-room—and try whether any further manifestations would be made there. We did so ; but all remained quiet. We then returned to the room we had just quitted, and sat down at another table covered with

---

* "New York Sun," August 27th, 1875.

a cloth. We had previously heard a rustling sound about and under the tables—such a sound as would be made by a person moving about in a heavy garment. This noise was accompanied by a scratching on the wood of the table, as though some one were scraping it with his nails. We then distinctly saw the cloth on the side of the table next to me move up, as though a hand raised it from beneath. The spirit being 'adjured in the name of the Holy Trinity to leave us,' the demonstrations ceased." Such rubbish as this Home gives in verification of "the nature and extent of the manifestations at that time."

> "Such intimate way,
> Close converse, frank exchange of offices,
> Strict sympathy of the immeasurably great
> With the infinitely small, betokened here
> By a course of signs and omens, raps and sparks—
> How does it suit the dread traditional text
> Of the 'great and terrible name'?
> Shall the Heaven of heavens
> Stoop to such child's play?"

At Florence in February, 1856, the impecunious "Seer" —now in the shade—joined the retinue of Count B——, a Polish nobleman, who had pressed the "mystic" one to accompany him to Naples. Thither, accordingly, they went; and Home met Robert Dale Owen, at that time American Minister at the Court. From Naples to Rome, —"to Rome" literally, for here Home abjured the Congregationalism in which he had been reared, and was received into the Roman Catholic Church.* The Pope, it is said, after questioning him as to his past life, significantly pointed to a crucifix, saying, "My child, it is upon that we place our faith."

---

* Home was confirmed upon Easter Monday, 1856, in the chapel of the English College, Rome.

June, 1856, brought the mystic being—now in the sunshine—to Paris, where he was presented to the Emperor and Empress, and where he first got into trouble with the Church he had so recently joined, in consequence of his continued dealings with "the spirits." After a run through France and Italy, and into Holland, the early part of 1858 found Home at St. Petersburg, where, still in the best society, he was betrothed to "Sacha" (a pet name), youngest daughter of the General Count de Kroll of Russia, and a goddaughter of the late Emperor Nicholas, to whom the lady's father was aide-de-camp. The marriage took place on Sunday, August 1st, 1858, in the private chapel attached to the house of the lady's brother-in-law, the Count Gregoire Koucheleff Besborodko — Alexander Dumas journeying from Paris to be present at the wedding. What more natural than the great French master of fiction honouring the Scottish-American romancer? The lady, taking the surest way "to make *Home* happy," in due course presented him with a son—Gregoire—who, in his infancy, was a medium, though we learn without regret that he has since "given up many indications of being a *seer*."

In 1862 Home was left a widower, his wife dying on the 3rd of July at the Château Laroche, Dordogne, France. After this he found his way to Rome, "to pursue his studies as a sculptor;" but the Pontifical Government being suspicious that he intended "chiselling" in the "Black Art" also, he was expelled the Roman territory. Upon Home's return to England, this matter was brought before the House of Commons by Mr. Roebuck, who contended that Home, as one of Her Majesty's subjects, was entitled to protection abroad, though he (Mr. Roebuck) had "no feeling for Mr. Home's profession further than having a contempt for the whole thing." Mr Layard replied that the mystic being having infringed the law of Rome, there was no cause for the interference of the Government; and so the subject dropped.

The "Seer" now settled down to work in earnest. In 1866 he delivered "lectures" in London, at one of which he was sketched for the benefit of the readers of "All the Year Round." The style will be recognized by most persons as "the touch of a vanished hand."

"On Thursday, the Fifteenth of February," says the writer, "I attended Willis's Rooms to hear the apostle preach; but before I could bring myself under the influence of the New Gospel, I was called upon to pay ten shillings and sixpence. 'Are there no five-shilling seats?' I asked. The answer was 'No, they are all gone; only a few half-guinea seats left.' I paid my half-guinea, and entered the room, and found that there were plenty of five-shilling seats vacant, but only a few half-guinea ones. On coming out I accused the man at the door of having (to use the mildest term) deceived me. He did not deny it, but said in excuse that it was not his fault—he had been told to say there were no five-shilling seats.

"I will relate briefly what I heard and saw, and what was the impression left upon my mind.

"As Mr. Home takes credit for being a medium, with extraordinary powers of body and mind, he can scarcely object to a description of his person. He is a tall, thin man, with broad, square shoulders, suggestive of a suit of clothes hung upon an iron cross. His hair is long and yellow; his teeth are large, glittering, and sharp; his eyes are a pale grey, with a redness about the eyelids, which comes and goes in a ghostly manner as he talks. When he shows his glittering, sharp teeth, and that red line comes round his slowly-rolling eyes, he is not a pleasant sight to look upon. His hands were long, white, and bony, and you knew, without touching them, that they were icy cold. He stooped over his paper, and rarely looked up, except to turn his eyes towards heaven in an appeal to the Deity.

"The first part of the lecture was very dull and heavy, being all about the indestructibility of matter. Before this 'head' was exhausted, I counted fifteen members of the congregation who were fast asleep. After my experience at the pay-place, it was rather startling to hear Mr. Home disclaiming all mercenary motives, and declaring that he had never received and never would receive money for his work. In a private circular to his friends he says, 'I need not tell you how important it is to me to have the support of my friends, not only as a comfort and encouragement to me, but as essentially aiding the cause in which they and I are deeply interested. Much, indeed, of *my own fortune*'" (Home says this should be *future*) "'must depend on the issue of this experiment.' I leave the reader to reconcile this appeal with his disavowal of mercenary motives how he or she can.

"It was a contradiction to deny the truth of spirit-rapping, when every Sunday, in church, we declared our belief in the communion of saints. Such was the argument. . . Now, what is the doctrine which Mr. Home propounds, and all these people subscribe to as a new article of faith? Boldly this: that Spiritualism, founded upon table-rapping, rope-tying, and banjo-playing in a cupboard, is *a means of man's salvation!* These are Mr. Home's own words."

About this time Home had thoughts of going upon the stage [*] (what a loss the slowly-rolling eyes with the ghostly rims must have been to the profession!), but in the latter

---

[*] Home gave "Readings" in the Queen's Concert Rooms, Hanover Square, so late as April and May, 1870.

end of 1866 something else turned up, in the form of the Spiritual Athenæum, of which he became secretary. Mr. Jenckens—Mr. Home's fast friend—was the honorary treasurer of this institution, and to him we are indebted for many stories of extraordinary manifestations, of which I give a specimen:

"Home, seating himself at the piano, performed with wonderful execution; then rising from the piano, he walked three or four times round our circle, mesmerizing each in turn. Here the extraordinary manifestations of elongation and shortening occurred. The height he attained must have been quite six feet nine inches; as he lengthened out, his clothing at the waist separated full six inches, and again, as he became shorter and shorter, the waistcoat descended quite down to his hips, Mrs. —— holding the end of his waistcoat to make certain of the elongation." What a charming picture this would have made! On another occasion Mr. Jencken—who is quite as circumstantial as a Court Jenkins—reports that Home said, "I am going to be elongated. Daniel will be elongated thirty times during his life. This is the sixth time." The fervid disciple also describes the fire test. Home, "passing up to the hearth, placed his hands and then his face in the flames and on the burning coals. . . . A lady present, unable to resist her expressions of alarm as his face neared and closed upon the flames, was reproved. Mr. Home, extending towards her his right hand, which had now become white and luminous, in reproachful warning saying, 'Have you no faith, no faith? Daniel will take no harm.'"*

---

* On one occasion Home allowed a gentleman to touch the burning coal he held, when the latter drew back, exclaiming, "By Jove, it *is* hot!" Home said the spirits sent a stream of some force down his hand and arm to counteract the influence of the heat!

"Miracle," says Goethe, "is the pet child of Faith," and Mr. Jencken, a perfect mountain of faith, is ready to vouch for any miracle and to stand by "Daniel" to the last gasp. It is remarkable that these very wonderful manifestations never took place save in the presence of the faithful few. Speaking of Home's exhibitions generally, "Fraser's Magazine"* remarks that the manifestations were "invariably of the same character, and became strong or weak in exact proportion to the abundance or lack of faith in the company. The greater wonders were never attempted, at all events they never succeeded, with an unbeliever in the room." On the faithful "Mr. Home exercised an influence strikingly analogous to that of Joe Smith over the earlier Mormonites.

"This worthy, it will be remembered, in profane imitation of a Scripture miracle, undertook to walk across a broad and deep river dryshod. His disciples were waiting in anxious expectation on the brink, when he inquired of them if they believed he could do it? They answered 'Yes.' 'Then,' said he, 'it's the same as if I had done it.' And they went on their way, rejoicing in their prophet and unshaken in their faith.

> 'And they believe him! Oh, the lover may
> Distrust the look which steals his soul away;
> The child may cease to think that it can play
> With heaven's lightnings; alchemists may doubt
> The shining gold the crucible gives out;
> But faith, fanatic faith, once wedded fast
> To some dear falsehood, hugs it to the last.'

"Mr. Home beats Joe Smith hollow, for he persuades people that they hear what they do not hear, that they see what they do not see, that an accordion, which makes an

---

* Vol. LXXI., 1865.

irregular noise, is playing a popular tune, and that he is floating near the ceiling when he is simply standing on his chair with one foot touching a disciple's shoulder.

"We once sat through a long *séance* with four or five other persons, and what struck us most was their mental condition during the entire performance. It fairly staggered us, till our observation was confirmed by friends who had noted the same phenomena at similar sittings. He did nothing but what might obviously and easily be done by hand and foot, for the whole of the so-called manifestations took place under a table of limited dimensions, with a green cloth lapped over the edge, which we were warned on no account to lift. After two hours spent in shaking and slightly raising the table, ringing the bell, sounding the accordion, twitching ladies' petticoats, pinching their knees, &c., &c., there was a pause of twenty minutes to rest Mr. Home or the spirits. We then resumed our seats, and remained nearly half an hour in solemn expectancy of the appearance of the spirit of Cagliostro, when the lights were to be extinguished, flowers were to be showered on us from unseen hands, and Mr. Home was to be wafted into the air.

"Unluckily the spiritual ladder was broken and the promised scene marred by an indiscreet suggestion to the effect that unless a spirit—like Sir Boyle Roche's bird—could be in two places at once, Cagliostro might be prevented from coming by a prior engagement for that night.

"Owing to this and two or three other signs of unbelief from the same quarter, the sitting was suddenly broken up, and we are obliged to rely on the account given in the 'Cornhill Magazine,' July, 1860, and confirmed by Dr. Gully, of the ordinary crowning exploit of the night.

"Darkness was declared to be an indispensable condition of the ascent; and when the lamps and candles were extinguished, a pale light still came in from the window, which it was the first business of the spirits to exclude. 'Presently the tassel of the cord of the spring blind began to tremble. We could see it plainly against the sky, and *attention being drawn to the circumstance,* every eye was on the tassel. Slowly, and apparently with caution or difficulty, the blind began to descend: the cord was evidently being drawn; but the force applied to pull down the blind seemed feeble and uncertain. It succeeded, however, at last, and the room was thrown into deeper darkness than before. But our vision was becoming accustomed to it, and masses of things were growing palpable to us, although we could see nothing distinctly. Several times, at intervals, the blind was raised and pulled down; but capricious as the movement appeared, *the ultimate object seemed to be to diminish the light.*'

"The simplicity of this observation is beyond all praise, and sufficiently indicates the mental state of the writer. After describing, with equal *naïveté*, the ringing of the bell, the pressure of hands, &c., he arrives at the *chef-d'œuvre:*

"'Mr. Home was seated next to the window.[*] Through the semi-darkness his head was dimly visible against the curtains, and his hands might be seen in a faint white heap before him. Presently he said, in a quiet voice, "*My chair is moving; I am off the ground: don't notice me; talk of something else,*" or words to that effect. It was very difficult to restrain the curiosity, not unmixed with a more serious feeling, which these few words awakened; but we talked *incoherently* enough upon some indifferent topic.'

---

[*] A suspicious circumstance, when we think of the efforts made to exclude the light.

"In other words, they fell into the trap laid for them, and suffered their attention to be distracted. He proceeds:

"'I was sitting nearly opposite to Mr. Home, and saw his hands disappear from the table, and his head vanish into the deep shadow beyond. In a moment or two more he spoke again. This time his voice was in the air above our heads. He had risen from his chair to a height of four or five feet from the ground. As he ascended higher, *he described his position*, which at first was perpendicular, and afterwards became horizontal. He said he felt as if he had been turned in the gentlest manner, as a child is turned in the arms of a nurse. In a moment or two more he told us he was going to pass across the windows, against the grey silvery light of which he would be visible. We watched in profound stillness, and saw his figure pass from one side of the window to the other, feet foremost, lying horizontally in the air. He spoke to us as he passed, and told us he would turn the reverse way and re-cross the window, which he did. . . . . He hovered round the circle for several minutes, and passed this time perpendicularly over our heads. I heard his voice behind me in the air, and felt something lightly brush my chair. It was his foot, which he gave me leave to touch. Turning to the spot where it was *on the top of the chair*, I placed my hand gently upon it, when he uttered a cry of pain, and the foot was withdrawn quickly, with a palpable shudder. It was evidently not resting upon the chair, but floating; and it sprang from the touch as a bird would. He now passed over to the farthest extremity of the room, and we could judge by his voice of the altitude and distance he had attained. He had reached the ceiling, upon which he made a slight move, and soon after descended and resumed his place at the table.'

"It thus appears that neither this gentleman nor Dr. Gully saw Mr. Home in the air. They merely saw and heard things from which they drew the inference that he was floating above and about them, as he said he was, the only palpable or material things being the passing and re-passing of an opaque substance, which they believed to be his body, across the window. It would be difficult, they urge, for Mr. Home to produce this effect, or to mislead them as to his whereabouts in the darkness, by his voice; but would it not be more difficult for him to suspend the law of gravitation, night after night, for the gratification of the curious? And why should we accept as a miracle that which had every outward and visible semblance of a deception?"

Lord Lindsay's celebrated story of Home's levitation will not be out of place here. His lordship wrote:

"I was sitting with Mr. Home and Lord Adare and a cousin of his. During the sitting Mr. Home went into a trance, and in that state was carried out of the window in the room next to where we were, and was brought in at our window. The distance between the windows was about seven feet six inches, and there was not the slightest foothold between them, nor was there more than a twelve-inch projection to each window, which served as a ledge to put flowers on.

"We heard the window in the next room lifted up, and almost immediately after we saw Home floating in the air outside our window.

"The moon was shining full into the room; my back was to the light, and I saw the shadow on the wall of the window-sill, and Home's feet about six inches above it. He remained in this position for a few seconds, then raised the window and slided into the room, feet foremost, and sat down.

"Lord Adare then went into the next room to look at the window from which he had been carried. It was raised about eighteen inches, and he expressed his wonder how Mr. Home had been taken through so narrow an aperture. Home said (still in a trance), 'I will show you;' and then, with his back to the window, he leaned back, and was shot out of the aperture head first, with the body rigid, and then returned quite quietly."*

The foregoing letter was thus ably dissected by the "Quarterly Review:" †

"1. Though it might have been expected that in narrating a marvel so astounding, Lord Lindsay would have been careful to state every particular that could be reasonably asked for, and to support his account of it by the testimony of other gentlemen by whom it was witnessed, he commences as if he were narrating the most ordinary occurrence, which ought to be received on his testimony alone—thus showing that he had previously surrendered himself unreservedly to the belief in Mr. Home's 'occult' powers, and that his testimony is therefore to be received with the gravest suspicion.

"2. He commits the flagrant inconsistency of telling us that whilst he and two other persons were 'sitting with Mr. Home,'—which, if words have any meaning, implies that Mr. Home was in the same room with him—Mr. Home '*was carried out of the window in the room next to where we were, and was brought in at our window.*'

---

* Clever spirits!—who
>   "' Mediums' raise by 'levitation,'
>   And subject them to 'elongation,'
>   And in and out of windows float them
>   Two stories high, lords vow—we quote them."
>   —*Punch.*

† "Spiritualism and its Recent Converts," October, 1871.

" 3. This spiritual transportation took place, not in open day, but *by moonlight*. If any wicked wag were to characterize Lord Lindsay's statement as *all moonshine*, would not the common sense of our readers accept the description ? "

Mr. Home's " levitation " seems to have been altogether of a doubtful character, but if accomplished, it need not therefore be ascribed to a spiritual agency, as I have demonstrated at the Egyptian Hall.

When Mr. Addison (who was claimed as a medium by the Spiritualists) offered Home £50 if he could float in the air in his presence, he declined the challenge, as he had the Emperor Napoleon's proposal for Robert Houdin to be present at one of his *séances*.

As to this man, of about eleven stone weight, being suspended in mid-air, like Mahomet's coffin, and " shooting " through an open window, it is too much ! I fear "airy Daniel" will have to repair to that " Retreat for decayed Spiritualists—The *Home* for Idiots "*—to find any general acceptance of these stories.

But—

"The pleasure, surely, is as great
Of being cheated as to cheat,"

so Mr. Home and his disciples must have been in a state of beatitude; though it is indeed wonderful to note the easy credulity with which these latter accept the marvellous, who would naturally be suspicious and exacting enough in ordinary cases.

"Suppose
A poor lad, say a help's son in your house,
Listening at keyholes, hears the company
Talk grand of dollars, V-notes, and so forth,
How hard they are to get, how good to hold,

---

* "Punch," November 5th, 1864.

The Mystic Sensitive.

How much they buy,—if, suddenly, in pops he—
'I've got a V-note!' What do you say to him?
What's your first word which follows your last kick?
'Where did you steal it, rascal?'

    •   •   •   •   •   •   •

But let the same lad hear you talk as grand
At the same keyhole, you and company,
Of signs and wonders, the invisible world;
How wisdom scouts our vulgar unbelief
More than our vulgarest incredulity;
How good men have desired to see a ghost,
What Johnson used to say, what Wesley did,
Mother Goose thought, and fiddle diddle dee;
If he then break in with, 'Sir, *I* saw a ghost!'
Ah, the ways change! He finds you perched and prim;
It's a conceit of yours that ghosts may be:
There's no talk now of cowhide. 'Tell it out!
Don't fear us! Take your time and recollect!
Sit down first: try a glass of wine, my boy!
And, David (is not that your Christian name?)
Of all things, should this happen twice—it may—
Be sure, while fresh in mind, you let us know!'
Does the boy blunder, blurt out this, blab that,
Break down in the other, as beginners will?
All's candour, all's considerateness. 'No haste;
Pause and collect yourself. We understand!
That's the bad memory, or the natural shock
Of the unexplained *phenomena!*'" •

CHAPTER V.

"DANIEL" IN THE LYO.'S DEN.

The *Trials* of a "disinterested" Medium—A *Home* Ruler (of the Spirits) receives a *cheque*—A dead Lyon's Ghost—"Danny" and his "darling Mother"—"Home, sweet Home"—"Them high folks"—"Pickles is good!"—"Daniel" come to Judgment—The Ortonian Theory—A Song of the Day.

THE late Dr. Robert Chambers, editor of "Chambers' Edinburgh Journal" says of Home, that "he came forward with no conceivable end but to propagate a knowledge of what he regards as important truths;" but most of us remember the celebrated action brought by Mrs. Jane Lyon against Daniel Dunglass Home and William Martin Wilkinson (his attorney *) in 1867, which certainly seems to throw a *slight* doubt upon the gentleman's statement.

For the information of the juniors and to refresh the memory of others, I may mention that the lady (whose husband, Charles Lyon, of Wooth Grange, Bridport, Dorset, had died in 1859) resided, about the year 1866, in apartments at No. 18 Westbourne Place. Home at the same period was resident secretary, *with a salary*, at the

---

* A formal defendant.

Spiritual Athenæum, 22 Sloane Street,* which was supported by subscription. The action was brought to recover some £30,000, which, as the plaintiff affirmed, Home had received from her by fraud, and a writ of *ne exeat regno* being obtained, the defendant was lodged in Whitecross Street Prison.

It seems the lady had heard of Home as "the head Spiritualist," who would be able to bring her into communion with her deceased husband; accordingly, "being possessed of this desire," she paid her first visit to No. 22 upon the 3rd of October, 1866, and there saw the defendant, sat at a table in his sitting-room with him, and heard raps which Home explained as a message from her late husband, read by aid of the spirit alphabet. The lady was so much pleased with the communications then received, that she requested the "medium" to call upon her the next day, when he should receive a cheque for £10 as a "subscription." Home (of course!) went, and after eliciting another message from the dead Lyon, came away clutching a cheque for £30 instead of the £10 promised. Several meetings took place after this, and the lady's affidavit shall continue the narrative, which is, to say the least, suggestive of human credulity upon the one side, and the craft of no apprentice hand upon the other.

EXTRACTS FROM MRS. LYON'S AFFIDAVIT.

"4. On or about the 6th of October last, the said defendant again called upon me in Westbourne Place aforesaid, and I again received him alone in my sitting-room, and he commenced talking to me on the subject of his marriage with his deceased wife, and told me how happy

---

* By a strange coincidence Cagliostro lived in this street.

he had been with her, and he stated his intention of marrying again, but said that he should not marry a young lady, as he did not like young ladies, but was anxious to marry an elderly lady, and that he should make a very loving and affectionate husband ; and from these remarks and others which followed on the same subject, I then inferred, and now verily believe, that he intended to make to me proposals of marriage; but I told him that the subject was distasteful to me, and I silenced him upon it at once. Almost immediately afterwards raps came again, indicating, as the said defendant induced me to believe, and as I, in fact, believed, the presence of my husband's spirit; and the following word, or words as nearly as possible to the following effect, were (with other words) then spelt out in the manner before referred to, the said defendant repeating rapidly the letters of the alphabet, and stopping from time to time as raps came indicating the letters to be used : ' My own darling Jane —— . . . . I love Daniel' (meaning, as I understood, the said defendant); ' he is to be our son ; he is my son, therefore yours.'"

This sudden change of front from the position of lover to that of son, betokens a tactician of no mean order, and it had the desired effect ; for when, upon the 8th of October or thereabouts, Mrs. Lyon's deceased husband raps out through the medium that she is to adopt "Daniel" as her son, and "make over to him a sufficient sum from her funded property to bring him in £700 a year," the silly lady proceeds to carry into effect what she conceives to be her husband's will, by transferring the value of some £24,000 sterling in stock to Dr. Chambers' "disinterested" *protegé*. But not content even with this, the rapacious "Seer," about the beginning of November, whilst *in a trance state* (he was wide awake to his own interests !) dictates word for word instructions for a will, whereby he is to take the arms and name of Lyon and *all the property!* This will was subsequently made by W. M. Wilkinson, of Lincoln's Inn Fields, the solicitor, and attested by Dr. Hawksley, of 70 Brook Street, Hanover Square, and Mr. Alexander Henry Rudall, a merchant, of 8 and 9 Great Tower Street, City, all intimate friends of the "disinterested" medium.[*] The eyes of the lady not being yet open to this gigantic imposition, about December the spirit alphabet is again in requisition, this time commanding that "Daniel" shall receive a present of £6,000 upon his birthday, which sum is also forthcoming by the transfer of £6,798 17s. 4d. Consolidated Bank Annuities into the name of Daniel Dunglass Home. Then, after a little mortgaging transaction, the poor lady, *minus* a considerable portion of her wealth, suddenly awakens from *her* trance, and in her affidavit continues:

"18. I have lately upon reflection become convinced that I have in the several transactions, matters, and things hereinbefore referred to, been altogether imposed upon by and made the dupe of the said defendant, Daniel Dunglass Home; and that the several directions, which at the time I believed to have been given as aforesaid by the spirit of my said late husband, were not in reality so given, but that they without exception emanated entirely from the said defendant and not otherwise."

In his affidavit in reply, Home proceeds to contradict the statements of Mrs. Lyon, whom he describes as a vulgar woman, the illegitimate daughter of a Newcastle tradesman, who speaks of "them high folks"—the Emperor of

---

[*] It is but fair to say that no fraud was imputed to Mr. Wilkinson, or either of the gentlemen who attested the "will."

Russia, &c. She is, in fact, according to her pseudo son "Daniel," a female tuft-hunter—though surely not more so than "her dear boy" who never tires of parading a considerable list of "high folks" of his acquaintance.

Now, Mrs. Lyon does not appear to have been a loveable lady by any means, and "Daniel" says that she was constantly and unpleasantly sighing for "Home, sweet Home." Yet, withal, he was desirous of changing his name to hers, and of becoming her adopted son. Could he have done all this from mercenary motives? Perish the thought! No, "Daniel;" did not Dr. Chambers vouch for you being above that sort of thing!

The case came before Vice-Chancellor Giffard, and occupied ten days in hearing, from the 21st of April to the 1st of May, 1868. For the plaintiff appeared Mr. W. M. James, Q.C., Mr. Druce, and Mr. Fischer; for the defendant, Mr. E. E. Kay, Mr. Matthews, of the Common Law Bar, Mr. Godfrey Lushington, and Mr. Fitzroy Kelly.

The Court was crowded to overflowing upon each of the days, the number of ladies being particularly noticeable. When leaving the Court upon the second day, the defendant was hooted by the crowd assembled outside; indeed, public feeling ran high against this prophet of the newest and most profitable dispensation.

The trial was not devoid of amusing features, for a titter ran round the Court when Home declared that he was of "a very nervous organization;" and a feeling of disappointment was manifest—especially among the daughters of Eve present—when the "mystic one" declined Mr. James's request that he should there and then give some specimen "raps" in the witness-box.

But Mrs. Lyon was a "treat!" It all came out how she had discovered "Danny's" wickedness by consulting the "sperrits" addicted to Miss Berry, in this wise:

MRS. LYON. Are there any sperrits here that knows me?
SPERRIT. Yes.
MRS. LYON. Who?
SPERRIT. Charles.
MRS. LYON. Is it my husband's sperrit, Charles Lyon?
SPERRIT. Yes.
MRS. LYON. Do you know of this business with Daniel Home?
SPERRIT. Yes.
MRS. LYON. Do you approve of it?
SPERRIT. No; it is an imposition.
MRS. LYON. What shall I do?
SPERRIT. Go to law at once. Be firm and decided.
MRS. LYON. Was your sperrit ever with Daniel?
SPERRIT. No, never.

This settled the business, and the lady *had* gone to law; and her "dear boy," whom she had warned to take care of his health, and had hinted to that end that "pickles is good," was now "a spiritual adventurer," "a poor sickly creature," and "a greedy, fawning, sneaking, *lieing* hypocrite;" and his son (then eight years of age) a rude, impertinent, "contradictious" boy.

Mr. W. M. James, Q.C., in his reply remarked that "the defendant was a young man, an adventurer, according to his own showing, exercising no trade or profession, and with no means whatever of living, except this singular gift of which he claimed to be in possession. It was, indeed, made matter of boast that he never took money or any fee for the exercise of his spiritual powers. It was quite clear, however, that it was to the possession of this peculiar gift that he owed any position, rank, or means of livelihood that he enjoyed."

The Vice-Chancellor, in his decree,* said he had read

---

* May 22nd, 1868.

the defendant's statements and explanations, and was altogether dissatisfied with them. "There must, therefore," he added, "be a declaration in the usual form, that the gifts and deeds are fraudulent and void. . . . The system (Spiritualism), as presented by the evidence, is mischievous nonsense—well calculated on the one hand to delude the vain, the weak, the foolish, and the superstitious; and on the other to assist the projects of the needy and the adventurer. Beyond all doubt there is plain law enough and plain sense enough to forbid and prevent the retention of acquisitions such as these by any 'medium,' whether with or without a strange gift; and that this should be so is a public concern, and—to use the words of Lord Hardwicke—of the highest public utility."

So "Daniel" found himself pitted against his "darling mamma" Lyon in the British Lion's Court of Chancery, and did *not* come out scathless. Indeed, the aged Lyon made "small bones" of her "Danny," who retired discomfited. But he had run through the *gamut* of "flats" and "naturals," and (unlike some of the *genus* "medium," who manage to secure "more kicks than halfpence") had gained a competence, so Mr. Howitt tells us, by his shows; which only proves the truth of the Ortonian theory — stolen from Miss Braddon's "Aurora Floyd"—that surely "people as has plenty money and no brains was made for them as has plenty brains and no money."

"Punch," then as ever pretty right, has a laughable rap at "airy Daniel," which is too true to have been pleasant to that mystic and sensitive being.

HOME, SWEET HOME!
(A Song of the Day.)

THROUGH realms Thaumaturgic the student may roam,
And not light on a worker of wonders like HOME!

CAGLIOSTRO himself might descend from his chair,
And set up our DANIEL as Grand Cophta there—
    HOME, HOME, DAN HOME,
    No medium like HOME!

Confronted with HOME, LYON's terrors are vain;
Into fortune he flies, and won't fly out again;
And with raps' worth as his, "worth a rap" means worth al'
For which, on rappees, up-to-snuff rappers call—
    HOME, HOME, DAN HOME,
    No medium like HOME!

Spirit-legs, spirit-hands, he gives table and chair;
Gravitation defying, he flies in the air;
But the fact to which henceforth his fame should be pinned,
Is his power to raise, not himself, but the wind!—
    HOME, HOME, DAN HOME,
    No medium like HOME!

He is vouched for by friends, F.R.S.'s, M.P.'s,
With EMP'ROR and CZAR hobs-and-nobs at his ease;
And to show off for shillings he cannot have grounds,
Who has still on tap drafts for thousands of pounds!—
    HOME, HOME, DAN HOME,
    No medium like HOME!*

---

* "Punch," May 9th, 1868.

CHAPTER VI.

THE JUGGLING GEMINI!

Buffalo Boys—Dancing Crockery—"George Brown"—"Making tracks"—An unfortunate Investigator—A "dare-devil"—Crossing the "Herring Pond"—The Gemini in London—"Punch" and the "Boys"—Discoveries and Exposures—"Fresh fields and pastures new."

IRA ERASTUS and William Henry Davenport were born at Buffalo,—a city in New York State, at the outlet of Lake Erie, on the Niagara River, and some twenty miles south of the celebrated "Falls"—the former upon September 17th, 1839, the latter upon the 1st of February, 1841. Their father, Ira, who was "in the police department," was a native of the same State, but said to be descended from early English settlers; their mother, whose maiden name was Virtue Honeysett, was born in Kent.

The boys had to "rough it" a little in their native town, and when we need first notice them particularly, were engaged in the unspiritual occupation of newspaper delivery. While they were still only children the "Rochester knockings" commenced, and, doubtless, from their employment, they were well posted-up in all the latest "phenomenal developments," as the newspapers of the day were teeming with such rubbish. When Ira had reached the age of fifteen, Davenport *père*, "from information received," was led to believe that his sons and daughter possessed the spiritual afflatus, and this conviction acquired confirmation by several startling feats performed by these children which received much attention from the curious and the credulous.

Accordingly the "Boys," having made a fair start, soon became adepts in the arts of deception. Rappings were now of frequent occurrence in the Davenport household, and contributed not a little to the Davenport income. For though the head of the family had felt some natural diffidence (especially natural in a gentleman attached to "the police department") at receiving money, he had been *induced* to do so; and we can well imagine the struggle it would cause him.

When any particular manifestations were about to take place, "a request was made, by means of the rappings, that the room should be partially darkened," says their faithful biographer, T. L. Nichols, M.D., and he continues: "It is perhaps useless to ask why. In nature and in art some operations require light and some its absence." But these "manifestations" were not ascribed to nature. Could they be to art? Presently Ira began to fly about the premises, and in this accomplishment he was quickly followed by William and their only sister Elizabeth Louisa, aged ten*—one of the original "Buffalo Gals;" and once (all this on the authority of the faithful and veracious Nichols!) †

---

* Who, as Mrs. E. Davenport Collie, in conjunction with Mrs. M. A. C. Lamb, has kept Yankeedom *au fait* in spirit rope-tricks during her brothers' absence in Europe.

† There is another biography of the Davenports by Orrin Abbott. It contains little worth recording save this remarkable and truly American couplet:
"When nightfall hangs her curtains high,
And starlight pins them to the sky"!

Ira was carried through the air from a room, and landed in the street, a distance by measurement of seventy feet. Also when the family were seated at breakfast, it was not an unusual occurrence for the knives, forks, and dishes (*déjeûner à la fourchette!*—the family prospects *were* looking up!) to commence a waltz, and the table to dance a jig—ending with a graceful *pirouette* in the air!

"The *séances* now began to be held regularly"—(of course!) "Loud raps were heard; the table answered questions; spectral forms were seen in the flash of a pistol; lights appeared in the upper parts of the room; musical instruments floated in the air, while being played upon, above the heads of the company. . . . While every person in the room was sitting by the tables in the darkness, the door of a pantry was flung violently open, and the entire stock of family crockery and glassware taken from the shelves and piled upon the tables. . . . Then the boys were raised up and placed upon the dishes, and all the chairs heaped up on the whole, without the agency of any mortal hand that could be discovered."*
We are carefully informed, you see, that all this took place in *total darkness*, though our friend Nichols might have left so much to the imagination of his readers. Then a message came from the spirit of one "George Brown," and Ira, "in the trance state," spoke as proxy for "George"—curdling the blood of the assembled Buffalonians by an account of how he had been murdered by robbers, known as the Townsend Gang, at a place called Waterloo. A few evenings after this, as Ira was delivering papers, he felt "queer," then lost his consciousness, and found himsel standing in the snow, with no tracks around him to show how he had come there, in a solitary place, a mile and a

---

* Nichols.

half from home, on the right bank of the Niagara River. "George Brown," at his next visit, declared that he had carried him across the river, which is half a mile wide, and brought him back again, just as an experiment; but as the boy was unconscious all the time until he found himself on the bank, while his family were getting alarmed at his absence, and as nobody saw him carried across the river, we have only "George Brown's" testimony on the subject, which we are not obliged to believe without a sufficient corroboration.

"Of course we cannot prove a negative. If the boy could be carried across the room and out into the street, why not across the Niagara River?—a feat beyond Blondin's, it must be confessed. If seventy feet, why not as many miles? If people lose their gravity, or are hurried away by their emotions or other sufficiently powerful influence, who shall say how far they may be carried?"[*] Who, indeed! Many persons will lose *their* gravity at the thought of Ira Davenport being "*hurried away by his emotions*, or other sufficiently powerful influence," to the opposite side of a river into "the untrodden snow," whence Ira doubtless "made tracks" (to use the elegant phraseology of his country) with a vengeance! Even the "Boys'" gullible biographer cannot swallow all that "George Brown" gives to the world through that "passive" newsboy, Ira Davenport. Nichols says, "I believe simply that Master Ira, as he said, and still says, in a manner that carries conviction with it, found himself standing in the snow on the bank of the Niagara, without knowing how he came there. As 'we must draw the line somewhere,' I propose to draw it here. 'George Brown' may have wished to stretch it; or he wished, it may be, to see his murderers stretching lines of a different

---

[*] Nichols.

description." Ah! dear Nichols; you have managed to keep out of the spirit-world until now, and surely do not doubt this aërial flight of Ira's, seeing that every Spiritualist accepts as Gospel the story of that substantial Venus, Mrs. Guppy's (I beg pardon, Mrs. Guppy-Volckman's) moonlight transit from Ball's Pond to Lamb's Conduit Street. But we must not imagine that all these statements rested upon the evidence of the Davenports alone. There were people to be found who would testify to the flying powers of the "Boys." Before a few "believers" upon one occasion *in a darkened room,* Ira was lifted bodily into the air and floated close to the ceiling, and William, with an auctioneer hanging to his legs, is said to have been "raised up with such force that his head broke through the ceiling of lath and plaster." People heard the crash! Was not that sufficient proof? And there could be no mistake when, a light having been obtained, a hole was found in the ceiling!

The necessity of even *such* confirmation is done away with now, for Mrs. Guppy comes through the ceiling, leaving never a crack behind; and Home slips through a brick wall without disturbing the setting!

The fame of the "Boys Davenport" had by this time spread widely, and many persons came from New York (three hundred miles away) to investigate the phenomena. One of these, Mr. Barratt, a Swedenborgian minister, of the "City of Churches," Brooklyn, locked himself in a room with the "Boys," and upon the candle being extinguished, it was rubbed over his face to enable him, so the spirits said, "to swallow the truth"! and his hat, after being dipped in a tub of water, was thrust, dripping, upon his head.* *The minister was convinced!*

---

* Page 63 Nichols' "Biography."

Then the spirit of " John Hicks," the deceased brother-in-law of the elder Davenport, declared that he had been poisoned by his wife ; but when the body was exhumed, *no evidence was forthcoming to prove the truth of the "spirit" communication !* * Had the "dear boys" been reading that Cock Lane ghost story, think you ? Another spirit, Sir Henry Morgan, formerly a Governor of Jamaica, who— " though names are of no consequence "—wished to be known as " John King," ordered them to travel ; and as public feeling began to run high against them in Buffalo —though still making a profitable business out of their peculiar powers—they resolved to accept the prudent hint, and seek, like other media, a more extended field for their operations.

Thus, about the time Home landed in England (1855), they started upon their peregrinations through America with such "spiritual effects" as a fiddle, guitar, tambourines, trumpet, bells, &c., and the "structure," or cabinet, in which (or the darkness) the " spirits " only would " manifest." Their father acted as showman, shutting the doors of the " structure," and describing how the guitar floated round the room " a-thrumming of its strings ; " but they soon found the necessity of an abler *explicateur*, and—like the Poughkeepsie Seer—gave the " old man " the go-by.

At the little town of Phœnix they were arrested for giving a performance without a licence, and lodged in prison, where, the regulations not being very strict (they gave a *séance* in jail for the benefit of the warder), they managed to escape,† and believers accepted this as evidence of

---

* Murder will *not* "out" in a proper manner with the spirits. " Mrs. Kempe," in the Cock Lane ghost story ; the Foxs' " Pedlar," and " John Hicks," all fail when *proof* is required.

† No great difficulty in America, one would say, having " Boss " Tweed's "escape" in view.

spirit power, likening them to Peter, whose chains fell from his hands when "the angel of the Lord came upon him."

The Brothers did tolerably well for the first seven years of their journeying in America, and during the last three they created great excitement wherever they went.

But the hubbub was not to continue for much longer; their "drawing" powers soon began to wane in their native country—the Civil War proving more exciting than the spirit mania. So a raid was projected upon John Bull's breeches-pocket, and the strollers left New York, August 27th, 1864, to cross what Yankees call the "Herring Pond," and give Europe a taste of their quality.

At this time the "Band of Brothers" was five in number, consisting of Dr. J. B. Ferguson the lecturer, formerly an Independent minister, of Nashville, Tennessee, in whose hand the "juggling Gemini" were little better than tools; the "Boys Davenport" themselves; the so-called secretary named Palmer, also well known in America as an operatic and theatrical agent, and who really acted in that capacity for Ferguson and the Brothers; and William M. Fay, a "Buffalo Boy" of German parentage, who had previously been a check-taker to the "show," but, discovering the rope trick and becoming a great adept at the coat feat, had been retained for that, and as a second string in the cabinet business, in case of William Davenport's health breaking down.

The Brothers were remarkably alike, aged respectively twenty-five and twenty-three years. They had long black curly hair, broad but not high foreheads, dark eyes, heavy eyebrows and moustache, firm-set lips, and a bright keen Yankee look.

Their first public performances in England (which consisted simply of an adaptation of the old Indian rope trick —they had given up "levitation") took place at the Queen's

Concert Rooms, Hanover Square, and created great excitement—" Punch" calling the epidemic "the *tie-fuss* fever," and gazetting the Brothers as "*Ministers of the Interior, with a seat in the Cabinet*,"—also suggesting, *àpropos* of the American Civil War then raging, that Ferguson, Fay, and Palmer, though taken for Yankees, seemed more likely to be *Confederates!* Certain it is, England was completely taken aback for a time by the wonders presented by these jugglers, which puzzled even those who were not prepared to throw overboard the ballast of common sense, and go drifting, buoyed up by the wind-bag of Ferguson's rhodomontade about spirit power.

Of the Davenport performances I have to say that they were, and still remain, the most inexplicable ever presented to the public as of supernatural origin; and had they been simply put forward as feats of jugglery, would yet have awakened a considerable amount of curiosity, though certainly not to the extent they did. *They* " knew the ropes." *The false pretence brought the money;* and that it was such I think will be generally allowed to have been abundantly shown by Mr. Cooke and myself at the Egyptian Hall and elsewhere.

Still, the Brothers did more than all other men to familiarize England with the so-called *Spiritualism*, and before crowded audiences and under varied conditions they produced really wonderful feats. The hole-and-corner *séances* of other media, where with darkness or semi-darkness, and a pliant, or frequently a devoted assembly, manifestations are occasionally *said* to occur, cannot be compared with the Davenport exhibitions in their effect upon the public mind. True it is that this boldness sometimes led to detection, which taught other medial gentlemen never to *guarantee* anything, for the "power" became a "capricious" one immediately upon the Davenports' failure. The mediumistic crew, now, take your money and you *take your chance* of a manifestation. As some of the "faithful" still believe in the spirit power of the Brothers, it will be as well that I remind them of certain facts, and recall two or three exposures of their tricks.

First, as to facts: their friendly "power," as Mr. Punch suggests, was certainly the power of darkness, for *all their tricks* were hidden from the view of the audience, either by the cabinet doors being closed, or the gas in the hall turned down. To say the least, this antipathy of "spirits" to the light is extremely unfortunate! Then, given that the hands were once loosed, there was nothing done but could have been produced by any two men. The hands never came farther out of the "structure" than a man could thrust them; the strains of melody (?) did not suggest a spiritual origin; instead of the Brothers sitting "passive," as that solemn humbug — Ferguson — would have his audience believe, the performers were frequently much distressed by their exertions in getting free from the ropes; anent which "Punch" had the following conundrum:—Why are the Davenport Brothers like an opheclide? Because they are brazen and blown. Then, when the Davenports secured themselves, the manifestations were instantaneous; but, *when properly tied*, the spirits were frequently a long time before releasing them.

Now for one or two of the exposures of the clever "Boys." I have named my own, and I discovered the mode of effecting the trick in this wise: Being present at a morning cabinet *séance*, given by the Davenports at the Town Hall, Cheltenham, I was elected a representative of the audience, and by the accidental fall of a curtain, hung over a window to exclude the light, I got a key to the *knotty* problem, which I have ever since used with such effect to reproduce all the tricks of the Brothers, that Spiritualists are in the singular dilemma of either branding them as impostors, or of claiming Mr. Cooke and myself as mediums. The latter is the course usually adopted. One who enjoys the confidence of "the faithful," describing our rope-tying performance at the Crystal Palace, declared, "If this be conjuring, 'Othello's occupation's gone.' Spiritualism itself is at a discount."* And the venerable Father of English Spiritualists, Mr. Benjamin Coleman, considers us not only "adepts in the art of legerdemain," but also "very powerful mediums, who find it much more profitable to pander to the prejudices of the multitude by pretending to expose Spiritualism than by honestly taking their proper place in our ranks as spiritual media . . . . All inquirers who desire to study the psychological character of spirit manifestations should be recommended to visit Messrs. Maskelyne and Cooke, who have gone on practising them with a perseverance worthy of a better aim, and who are now, in my opinion, the best of living mediums for the production of *strong physical manifestations*. This statement, often repeated by me, has been met with the remark, 'but they themselves say they *are not* mediums;' as if what *they say* should influence the minds of any intelligent Spiritualist who sees *what they do*." †

The Brothers have failed to release themselves from the bonds on many occasions. At the "Modern Tyre," the Liver proved too knowing a bird to be taken in by their spiritual pretensions; and two local gentlemen commenced binding the Davenports so securely that Dr. Ferguson immediately stepped forward, and with a knife freed William's wrist, saying that the rope was cutting it. In confirmation, William held up his hand, down the back of which blood

---

* Mr. Algernon Joy, Secretary to the National Association of Spiritualists, in "The Spiritualist." May 15th, 1873.

† "The Spiritualist," October 10th, 1873.

was flowing, and then walked off the stage with his brother, who had been released.

Dr. Ferguson wished the audience to believe that the wound upon William's wrist had been caused by the severe tying—whereas it was obvious that he himself had inflicted a slight cut in releasing the performer. The excited crowd, now more sceptical than ever, scrambled upon the platform, and thrusting the reverend gentleman from Nashville, Tennessee, into the cabinet, turned it over upon him—much as the young bucks of the past treated the ancient "Charleys,"—and, in the end, the "structure" was smashed, and the pieces borne away as trophies.

Now, without palliating the lawlessness here shown, I must hold this to be a striking proof of the inability of the spirits to do anything for their *protégés*.

At Huddersfield, shortly after the Liverpool *fracas*, a similar exhibition took place; and in Ireland, at a private *séance*, Ira Davenport and William Fay were baffled by a gentleman whom they thought to be a Spiritualist; and after sitting an hour without manifestations, they were untied at their own request.

Numberless have been the exposures that the hands appearing at the apertures in the cabinet doors were those of the mediums—frequently by placing colouring matter upon the hands thrust out, and afterwards discovering the same upon the hands of the Brothers. But all this is as nothing to the genuine Spiritualist, who accepts the theory put forward in Hazard's "Mediums and Mediumship," which accounts for this by the colour being transmitted from the spirit-hand to the material one. So when the speaking trumpet is privately blacked, and after the spirit has spoken a mourning rim is found round the medium's mouth, that, doubtless, has been "transmitted"—and there an end!

After making a considerable sum of money out of the

credulity of the English people before the break-up, the Davenports took themselves off to "fresh fields and pastures new."

Since then the European continent has been much favoured by the "juggling Gemini."

CHAPTER VII.

OUR SPIRIT GUIDES.

Music Hall Ditties—Lindley Murray—A Fighting Spirit—A Dutch Ghost—Rifle *v.* Spirit (Mask)—" Mailed in the Iron Box "—Music of the Angels—" Home Quiet, Peace, and Blesséd Love ! "—A Harris-ing Picture.

OUR "spirit guides" have nothing of the staid and sober ghosts of our youth about them — the bad ones clanking their chains like old Marley — the good clothed in white robes, and with looks of "ineffable sweetness." The dreary annals of modern Spiritualism contain few spirits who behave with the propriety formerly supposed to attach to their order; indeed, the greater number now show signs of deterioration, and seem to find employment in singing music hall ditties, and, taken altogether, are either very stupid or very bad. Their names, or those they condescend to be known by, read as if copied from a play-bill; some, fanciful and fascinating as the *noms de plume* of your burlesque actresses, others redolent of the romance of the Adelphi or the vulgarity of the " Vic." We have rollicking Irishmen and Chinese philosophers, little girl spirits with osculatory propensities, and " Uncle Ben" dittos, who sing such charming ballads as "Old Dog Tray." There are some who denounce the rich as "them as has the dollars ;" and we have Druidic spirits with unpronounceable names; a ghostly "Sam Weller" attends upon a medium, whose "ordinary manifestations" are working a sewing-machine and playing upon a mouth-organ; and a " control," in answer to the question, "Are you the spirit of Lindley Murray?" shall reply, " I are," to the immense satisfaction of the faithful. There is a pugilistic spirit, too, ready to knock the truth into you, and "spreading confusion and dismay in the circle." This "fighter" has the full approbation of Mr. Burns, who considers that "we want more of them in both worlds; but it is our business that we make the right use of them. 'John King' was and is a fighter—a great fighter, never getting tired of his difficulties. 'Jack Todd,' the Liverpool spirit, was also a fighter. 'James Lombard' is not silky-fingered either; and the 'Peter' who controls Miss Showers will stand no nonsense. We would rather have a fighter, be he man or spirit, than one of your saintly white-fingered sneaks, who is always doing you a dirty turn when behind your back. The fighter is a man of honest courage, and there is something to be got out of him."*

Such are a few of the mysterious visitants from the borderland of another world. Strange to say, whatever their nationality, our ghostly *confrères* usually speak English in England, though it is seldom of the best! Should they venture upon their (supposed) native tongue, the spirits are often caught tripping.

Numberless are the errors of the "invisibles:" a story from New York tells how a Dutchman consulted the rappers, and instantly became a sceptic when the spirit of his wife returned answers to his questions in English instead of her own vernacular. Thus:

"Ish dat you, mine vrow?"

---

* "Medium," September 3rd, 1875.

"Yes, I am your *diseased* wife, who—"

"You do not shpeak ze trudth, ghost; mine vrow can talk noding bud Dudtch, and she not never said tearest in all her lifes. It vas alvays ' Haunts, you tief!' or ' Haunts, you shkamp!' Bah! you are not mine dear vrow!" So the poor Dutchman went away disgusted with the spirits, and disconsolate at receiving no tender message in her usual manner from his loving and lost spouse!

All the spirits, whether comic (as they frequently are) or sentimental, untruthful or veracious, bold, bashful, merry or lachrymose, are an inane lot, adding nothing whatever to the sum of human knowledge, and talking the dreariest twaddle. Their statements, also, are received with grave suspicion by Spiritualists themselves, who allow that many of the communications are frivolous and untruthful. Contrast Coleridge's thoughts

> "Of that innumerable company
> Who in broad circle, lovelier than the rainbow,
> Girdle this round earth in a dizzy motion,
> With voice too vast and constant to be heard;
> Fitliest unheard! for, oh ye numberless
> And rapid travellers! what ear unstunned,
> What sense unmaddened, might bear up against
> The rushing of your congregated wings?"

with the garrulous, lying, tricky, and vain denizens of the "spheres" of the "Spiritual" idea!

America, which usually sends us the raciest Spiritual and other news, has been excited by accounts of "shooting at a spirit" for a wager; and the St. Louis "Republican"[*] describes the new kind of target:

"There it was, a pale ghostly countenance, that looked as though it might have belonged to a girl of seventeen at some previous time in the world's history. It did not look

---

[*] August 10th, 1875.

a bit like real flesh and blood. Had it been possible to remove the front of the cabinet suddenly, one never would have expected to see any pinned-back gear about the nether portion of the materialization. It was a face that might have belonged to some Greek maiden two thousand years ago, and reminded one of the marble countenance of some statue. So much of the figure as was visible was suggestive of a lost collar-button a little lower down. All who saw were fairly transfixed with astonishment. The features were perfectly clear and distinct, being illuminated by a soft light. There was not the slightest movement of a muscle or an eyelid that could be distinguished. While all were eagerly gazing at the vision, there was an explosion that caused a rude interruption of the imaginative reveries the more superstitious had fallen into. . . Without the tremor of a muscle Cunningham fired, apparently thinking no more of shooting a couple of girls than a Comanche would. At the shot the face remained steadfast. It was not scared and did not wink. A few seconds it remained as before, and then the curtain mysteriously slid across and obscured it from view."

Now it seems all this can be easily accounted for. "*The spirits may bring veritable masks into the cabinet!*" Mr. Harrison observes: "On reading the account of the shooting at a spirit, I at once came to the conclusion that in all probability not one of Slade's masks but one of Clark's* masks was brought in by the spirits, fired at by Mr. Cunningham, and taken away again by abnormal agency, so that nothing was afterwards found in the cabinet.

"The questions at issue in this matter are serious enough, because the narrative, in the form in which it has been so

---

* Dr. Slade is a noted medium for mask effects. W. C. Clark was the "medium" in this case.

widely published, almost challenges disbelievers to shoot at materialized spirits; and if they do this at such *séances* as Mrs. Compton's, *a medium will be killed.* It is serious also if it proves that tricky spirits can show masks at *séances without the knowledge of the medium;* for if this took place when the medium had not been bound and searched so thoroughly as in the present instance, he would innocently be condemned as an impostor." *

I make no comment upon this: those who can accept the mask theory are past argument! Doubtless it would be awkward for other media than Mrs. Compton if the *séance* room were turned into a shooting gallery!

"Skiwaukie," an Indian chief, who has been about a century in the higher hunting-grounds, wrote a letter, directed the envelope, put a stamp on it, and "mailed it in the iron box at the street corner." Here is a facsimile of the address:

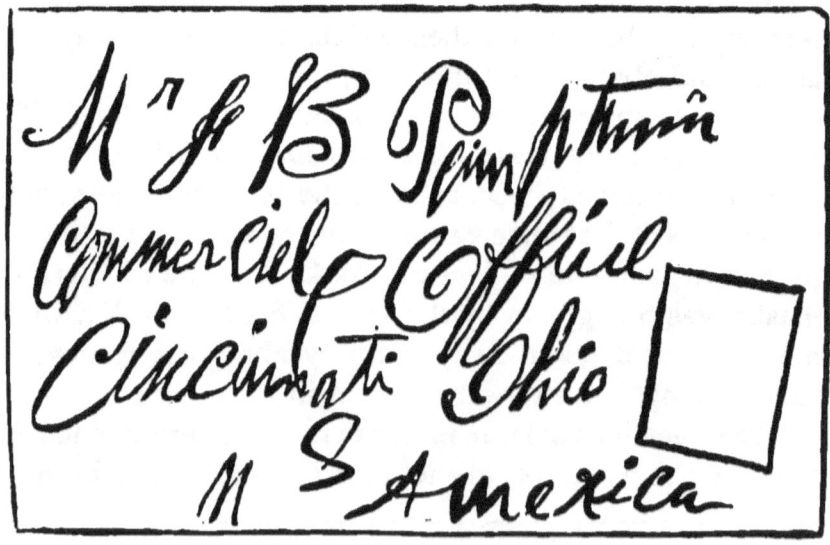

---

* "The Spiritualist," September 10th, 1875.

We have seen that the spirit-hand is a very shaky one; and they are as much behind in music as in writing. But one luminous star is said to irradiate the musical world with its lustre; for Mr. Jesse B. H. Shepard is reported to have suddenly commenced his "incomparable performances upon the piano" about 1868, without any previous tuition. It seems somewhat strange that we outsiders have heard so little of the fame of a gentleman who gives "the music of angels" to the world, therefore I must be excused for letting Mrs. Grundy know what a treat has been lost.

The "Washington Gazette" (December, 1868) is the oracle, and its words prove how poetical the Yankee penny-a-liner can be even in "this hard pragmatical age": "In a *salon*, where a dim religious light prevailed over shadows, all voices hushed, he sits, a nucleus of invisible shades. He seems a musical instrument himself, and, with the spirit of each composer, with his own peculiar style and *con amore*, strikes the beautiful white keys and makes the pianoforte that which only genius can make of an orchestra—one, in many instruments combined. We easily imagine ghostly outlined forms of Donizetti, Meyerbeer, Rossini, or Bellini bending over the sure and rapid fingers, in willing measures their brains outwrought on earth, or delighting in the expression of some exquisite and new combination." I hope all this is true; but my experience of spirit music has been limited to tambourines or concertinas, which seem to be the height of their ambition. If spirits rashly venture upon the guitar, the melody is usually a failure.

> "Suppose the spirit of Beethoven wants to shed
> New music he's brimful of? Why, he turns
> The handle of this organ, grinds with Sludge:
> And what he poured in at the mouth o' the mill

> As a thirty-third sonata—(fancy now!)—
> Comes from the hopper as a bran-new Sludge!—nought else:
> The Shaker's hymn in G, with a natural F,
> Or the 'Stars and Stripes' set to consecutive fourths."*

Indeed, the deterioration is noticeable in everything, but nowhere more so than in the "poems," which "the great ones gone for ever and ever by," are libelled with having written in the spirit-land. George Washington was not a poet, but we might expect something better than this to appear under an engraving of himself:

> "When the likeness of this portrait you see,
> Remember that it is to represent the likeness of me;
> But the spirit in its brightness you cannot see,
> For that is far above the likeness of thee."
> —G. WASHINGTON.†

Under the picture of Franklin in the same book we have the following lines composed in his "angel's home":

> "The likeness of this portrait is to represent
> The likeness of man when he dwelt here below;
> But the likeness of the spirit you would like to know,
> And this would be no more than I would like to show;
> But the mind is not prepared the likeness for to see
> Of the spirit in his angel's home as bright as we."
> —B. FRANKLIN.

And Rousseau, in the "Summer-land," has the following invocation:

> "O spirits! come, and let your power descend;
> The power shall come, and bless the world
> For ever without end!"
> —JEAN JACQUES ROUSSEAU.‡

Thus are the great ones treated by the Spiritualists! A literary ethereal being gives us a little—very little—*Light*

---

* *Sludge the Medium.*—R. B. Browning.
† From "Love and Wisdom in the Spirit-World." Particular attention is invited to this book by the "New York Spiritual Telegraph."
‡ "Medium," September 23rd, 1870.

from the spirit-world in an "Essay on Wisdom," to wit, "Wisdom is what is wise. Wisdom is not folly, and folly is not wisdom. Wisdom is not selfishness, and selfishness is not wisdom. Wisdom is not evil, and evil is not wisdom. All is not wisdom; all is not folly." We are also assured that "men are what they are," and that "change is alteration."

But the Spiritualists have an inspired poet and preacher, the Rev. Thomas L. Harris, whose "lyric," "The Golden Age," has been pronounced to have "scarcely less than Miltonic grandeur, while in parts, at least, it has more than Miltonic splendour." Here is some of it:

> "The thirst of knowledge never made men bad,
> 'T is self-conceit, wrapped in its long-eared skin
> Of most supreme content, that makes men base,
> Or, if it finds them base, to folly adds
> Insufferable vanity, that fain
> Would make their minds the measuring-rods of truth.
> Pouring the vast Atlantic through a straw
> Were wisdom to such madness. Oh, how vain
> Creed-building looks to free and cultured minds!"

More than Miltonic splendour indeed! In "earth-life," the great poet would not have dreamt, even in his grandest flights, of venturing upon such a line as

> "Pouring the vast Atlantic through a straw."

But in the spirit world hear how Milton is reported to speak for the "invisibles":

> "Although you cannot see us, we are everywhere,
> We creep gently o'er the carpet and softly up the stair!"*

The Rev. (Mrs.) Harris also startles the world with *Byron's Prophecy* concerning England:

> "There is a palsy on thy dying brain;
> There is a leprosy upon thy skin;

---

* "The Christian Spiritualist."

> O England, thy last prophet pleads in vain;
>   The seer Carlyle sits thy proud gates within,
> Reasoning with thee of righteousness, and sin,
>   And retribution—men believe him not.
> The rich more wealth, the great more greatness win:
>   The peasant grows a pauper, menial, sot;
> Lordlings drink, dice, and drab, fearing no Chartists' plot.
>
> "Yet wide and deep, from Mersey to the Thames,
>   The rankling evils of the social state
> Ripen to ruin. Hell's devouring flames
>   Burn in thy breast, while sleek red-tapists prate
> Of 'Progress,' and the Tory press cry 'Wait.'
>   France, now your friend, ere long shall be your foe.
> Your satraps feast with Cyrus at the gate;
>   Your wooden walls rot fast as April snow—
> The bull with gilded horns waits the destroyer's blow."

From this Harris-ing picture let us turn to the utterances of one "Pollok," through the reverend gentleman, entitled *The Doom of England:*

> "Let those fly to the mountains, where on high
> Throned Independence waves her flag of stars,
> Who prize home-quiet, peace, and blessed love.
> For, surely as the living God endures,
> The day of England's ruin draweth nigh."

I am almost inclined to doubt the inspiration of the Reverend Harris, when I find Columbia recommended for "home-quiet, peace, and blessed love!" Is the great American trance-speaker poking fun at us, think you? How long are we to endure such rubbish?

> "Milton composing baby-rhymes, and Locke
> Reasoning in gibberish; Homer writing Greek
> In noughts and crosses; Asaph setting psalms
> To crochet and quaver."*

When shall we have some decent work from the ghosts? Why should not the spirit of Homer solve the problem of

---

* *Sludge the Medium.*

his birth and life, and give the world a new poem in his classic Greek? Why leave the authorship of the Letters of Junius a mystery, when the spirit must be panting to give the truth to the world? Or is the "dead past" to give nothing up but miserable libels upon the memory of Shakspeare, Milton (not "*mute*," but inglorious enough!), Bacon, or of others whose names are written upon the great bead-roll of our illustrious dead?

CHAPTER VIII.

THE MEDIUMISTIC CRAFT.

What is a Medium?—Artemus Ward's idea of "Sperrit Rappers"—Dangers of Investigation—The "Spirits' Home"—Trance Media—Lying Oracles —Writing Media—Dot your "i's"—Spirit Painting—A Conference in Bloomsbury—Spiritual Quacks.

"IT seems desirable to define as far as possible what a 'medium' is, and how the phenomena are produced. A medium, then, is said to be a person whose body gives off a peculiar kind of magnetic *aura*, an invisible fluid, supposed to be the connecting-link between mind and matter, and through the agency of which the human spirit is supposed while in the flesh to control the physical body." This definition being taken from a "useful book for inquirers,"* having at one time received an affectionate pat upon its *back* from Mr. Burns, may be taken as "by authority." Certainly this has been weakened of late, since the publisher of Southampton Row veered round, and declared that "'Where are the Dead?' is like a pile of sandwiches in the form of a man, but not digested nor assimilated to the organic peculiarities of the form they take."†

---

* "Where are the Dead?"
† "The Medium," November 5th, 1875.

I consider Artemus Ward's description of a medium much the best, and give it in his own original style:

"Just so soon as a man becums a regular out and out sperret-rapper, he leeves orf working, lets his hare grow all over his face, and commensis spungin his livin out of other people. He eats all the dickshunaries he can find, and goze round chock full of big words, scarein the wimmin folks and little children, and destroying the piece of mind of every famerlee he enters. He don't do nobody no good and is a cuss to society, and a pirate on honest peple's corn beef barrils. Admittin all you say about the doctrine to be troo, I must say the reglar perfessional sperrit-rappers—them as makes a bizzness on it—air about the most ornery set of cusses I ever enkountered in my life."

It is generally understood amongst the faithful that the mediumistic power entails some heavy penalties upon the possessors. They are, it is said, "kittle cattle," "furiously jealous" of each other; they are "not remarkable, either, for intellectual or moral qualities;"* (I take this to mean that mediums are rather noted for the absence of those qualities, which is a fact), and they have "great temptation to recruit the bodily forces by stimulants." †

This is rather a gloomy state of affairs, especially when we remember that, in one out of every seven persons, the mediumistic power may be developed!

But let us suppose a medium "as chaste as ice, as pure as snow," without guile—neither ignorant, or uneducated, or drunken—can you place reliance upon his, or her, spirit message then? No! Andrew Jackson Davis very early in the movement discovered that it would never do to pin your faith to any medium. In his "Philosophy"

---

* Mr. S. C. Hall.
† "The Spiritualist," June 15th, 1873.

(page 91), he says, "*There is a certain class of unadvanced spirits* who, under peculiar circumstances, will say precisely what the questioning minds of the circle ardently, and therefore positively, require." Then there are certain spirits who, "when first materializing themselves, have often been obliged to take on somewhat of the features of the medium;" and others (bad ones these) who "have the power of materializing if they choose, or of showing the medium if they choose, and in both cases the medium is a helpless instrument in the hands of an inexorable power.*

At the first blush it would appear that there is no royal road to knowledge in this matter, considering the difficulties surrounding the investigation; for, though the Faithful admit the existence of bad mediums, they never name them, but the exposures that crop up from time to time are all put down to the machinations of evil spirits. Are lies told in the "circle"?— Bad spirits! Does the materialized form bear too striking a resemblance to the "passive"?—Bad spirits! Is the bull's-eye turned on too quickly, revealing the medium off his seat, and endeavouring to escape from his bonds?—Bad spirits! Is the sensitive being favoured by the "starry hosts" a drunkard?—Bad spirits, undoubtedly! So it is all through. Blind faith is the only "royal road,"—proof you cannot have. Beware even how you attempt to get it; for I will repeat a story which you may find in a little pamphlet † published under the auspices of the Spiritual Institution— *i.e.*, Mr. Burns!—showing the danger of experimentalizing.

"I was once," says the author, "present at a cabinet *séance* of the Eddy mediums, when, as usual, a committee was appointed to conduct the proceedings and see that

---

* "The Spiritualist."
† "Mediums and Mediumship," by Thomas R. Hazard.

there was no trickery or 'humbug' practised by the two brothers and sister mediums. There was a sceptical doctor put on the committee, who, I understood, had figured rather prominently before, and was chosen expressly on that account. The manifestations progressed as usual until a gigantic arm and hand, apparently of twice or thrice the magnitude of that of the lady medium, projected from the hole in the cabinet, whereupon the doctor (who had come prepared) let fly from a syringe a charge of writing-ink upon the outstretched arm. He then proceeded directly to the cabinet, and released the girl medium before she was apparently aware of his object; but no sooner was she before the audience than this 'self-styled accuser of mediums' grasped his victim by the arm, and dragging her forward on the platform, triumphantly exhibited the traces of her 'imposture and cheat' in unmistakable marks or stains of ink on the wrist. I shall never forget the scene that then transpired. There stood the medium, seemingly in blank amaze, not only convicted of fraud, but caught in the 'very act;' and there stood the burly doctor, elate with his victory, inasmuch as he had now proved his former accusations against the mediums true. But soon the scene shifted. Casting her eye on her 'accuser,' the medium seemed suddenly to realize and accept the situation, and seizing her 'exposer' by the nape of the neck, she sent him whirling around the platform as easily as a Hercules or Samson (with whose spirit she was perhaps possessed) could fling a cat. Nor could the hapless doctor in any way escape; for no sooner would he show the least indication to move, be it ever so stealthily, than the 'humbug' of a medium would dart tiger-like at him, and again send him flying around the stage . . . . At last, however, the doctor's beseeching looks seemed to prevail, and he was permitted to sneak quietly away."

Notwithstanding Mr. Hazard's jubilation at the doctor's painful position, he considered that a trick had been practised by the medium; but he got into *more experienced hands*, he tells us, soon after this, and became convinced that he was wrong.

The Eddys are said to be a great draw in "the States" now, and a Colonel Olcott* describes the ponderable ghosts at the Spirits' Home, Chittenden, Vermont; and they are very wonderful in the Olcottian narrative. English Spiritualists, however, do not care to take even the colonel's word without some corroboration, as the Eddys have not been above trickery before, and therefore Mr. Harrison puts

A PROBLEM.

"Colonel Olcott's book narrates how at one time the Eddy Brothers publicly exhibited genuine spiritual manifestations as conjurors' tricks, as has also been done by Melville Fay, Von Vleck, and some other physical mediums. What kind of spirits are they who aid mediums in such a career?"

Mr. Algernon Joy, Secretary of the *National Association of Spiritualists*, recently returned from America, reports a visit to the " Spirits' Home." He says:

"While there I saw no manifestations under test conditions. I firmly believe that every spirit that came out upon the platform was William Eddy himself; those that only showed in the doorway, the same on his hands and knees; and the small children that appeared were made-up dolls."†

---

* Of the New York "Daily Graphic," which does a "good thing" by illustrating the "materialization" of the Eddys.

† "The Spiritualist," Dec. 10th, 1875.

"There is a tide in the affairs of men," and the Eddys have taken it "at the flood." They ostensibly keep a farm (the house was specially built with a large "*séance* room" in it), and produce a fine crop of spirits, while a large flock of *geese* is regularly drawn from all parts of the States, to witness "manifestations" which the best friends of the cause must be ashamed of.

I must now advert to several forms of mediumship, and may commence with

TRANCE SPEAKING,*

which is a very ordinary form of mediumistic power, and any one with a ready wit and a glib tongue would seem to be fit for it; not so think the Spiritualists. Judge Edmonds† wrote that "the invisible intelligence takes possession of the mind of the medium, and compels his utterance of its ideas, in defiance of the will of the mortal through whom it is talking," and I am sorry to say the communications of these spirit friends are *not* to be relied upon. If the medium—"in the trance state"—happens, possibly by some hint obtained from yourself, to hit upon the truth or something like it, you are to accept that as a useful revelation from the spirits; but should the message not square with your own knowledge, ideas, or desires, there is an easy way out of the difficulty by laying all the blame upon bad spirits. You accordingly bind yourself to an oracle

---

* "Change Apollo into a spirit, and the Pythoness into an American girl, and you will have the trance medium."—SIGNOR MONTI.
† "Spiritualism," Vol. I., page 38.

which either speaks truth or untruth as you desire its communications shall be read. But how about the oracle that "lies like truth"? may not this be a Jack o' Lantern to lead you to destruction?

Usually the trance-speaking is very vapid stuff indeed; if not entirely colourless, "what is true is not new, and what is new is not true." Even Spiritualists themselves begin to see something of this. Mr. John Priest, Secretary of the Liverpool Psychological Society, who we find is "a recent adherent to the cause" (so he may have more discretion shortly), "dealt with what he considered to be serious objections to trance-speaking; one was Lindley Murray forgetting his grammar in controlling certain mediums, the remarkable sameness of Mrs. Tappan's orations, and want of book-knowledge, whether delivered by the supposed spirits of Judge Edmonds, Professor Hare, or A. A. Ballou."*

Before leaving this "head" I may give, in mellifluous Cora Lavinia Victoria's † own words, some of the wonders worked by those under the spiritual afflatus:

"Persons unlettered in the sciences or in the languages were made to speak other tongues than their own, and in philosophy and science transcended any possible knowledge or education. Direct individual intelligence controlled numbers of persons—they are now counted by the thousand—who spoke words during these states far transcending their ordinary culture, beyond any knowledge they had gained in schools; and in every instance these utterances *claimed to be dictated* by the spirit of some departed soul."

---

* "Spiritualist," Sept. 3rd, 1875.

† Mrs. C. L. V. Tappan—a trance speaker, who has predicted that St. Peter's Cathedral at Rome will be converted to a Temple of Spiritualism ere long!

I have yet to meet with those who have spoken beyond their "ordinary culture" whilst in the supposed trance. Instead of speaking foreign tongues, the usual medium—in trance or otherwise—is rarely master of his own.

Certainly the media frequently make statements "beyond any knowledge they have gained in schools" or elsewhere, for missing relatives who have been declared *by the spirits* to be dead, have had an awkward habit of turning up again in the flesh, and one lady, who received a communication through a medium to the effect that her son on his way down the Mississippi had, when the steamer took fire, jumped overboard and been drowned, returned home in great grief, and found the young man awaiting her arrival! But of course this was a lying spirit!

The electric telegraph had told the truth about the disaster to the steamer, but the "spirits" had guessed—and guessed wrong—about the lady's son.

WRITING MEDIA—*

—are those who give warnings of a personal and relative character, though entirely unconscious of the matter produced. This guidance of hands by the spirits (some, confessedly bad ones!) might produce awkward results. " Fraser's Magazine " † says : " If the spirits have such a power, there is an end of moral responsibility. The spirit of Jonathan Wild may slide a bishop's hand into an unsuspecting layman's pocket, or the spirit of Fauntleroy may commit a forgery with the pen of Mr. T. Baring or Lord Overstone."

See how " Ski," that educated old Indian, determined to

---

* " Some ghosts do, mortal hands compelling,
Write letters in *phonetic* spelling."—*Punch.*
† Vol. LXXI., page 42.

show his caligraphy to advantage, makes Mrs. Hollis the medium through whom he writes upon a slate *under a rug:*

("*Him be here and see you, Ski.*")

This was regarded as highly satisfactory; but Mrs. Hollis again placed the slate and paper under the rug; and the following communication was given, the spirit tapping with the pencil when he had finished. [See next page.]

These are fair specimens of spirit writings. They are invariably bad, being written by the medium under difficulties, sometimes beneath a rug, as in this case, or under a table, or with the medium's hands secured, when the pencil has to be held between the teeth.

After all, this writing under a rug is not half so wonderful

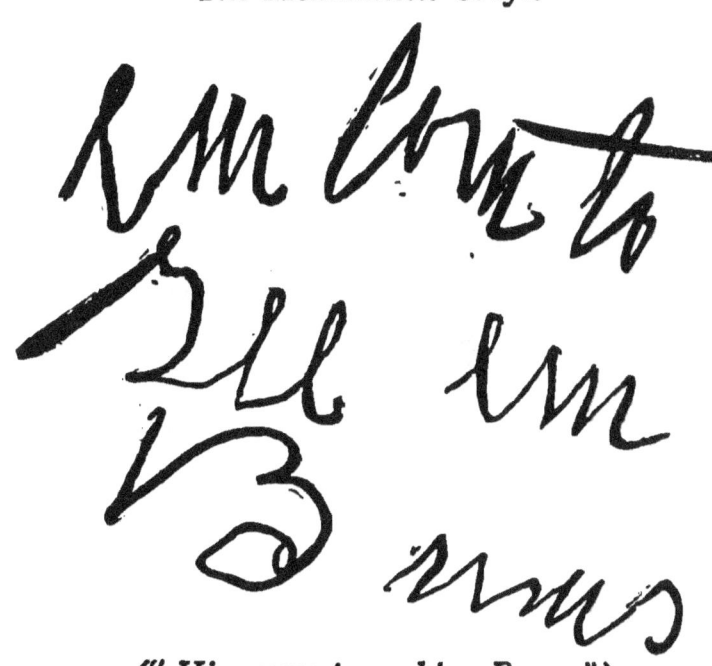

("Him come to see him, Burns.")

as that educated pen of the Davenports, which, after rising from the table and writing a message upon a slip of paper, retired "in soft confusion," but almost immediately returned *to dot an i* !

PAINTING MEDIA

are a terror to me. Many of the "spiritual" daubs would disgrace the artists who decorate our pavements with their chalk designs, and are only so far *spiritual* as to resemble nothing in nature, "either in the heaven above, or in the earth beneath, or in the waters under the earth." They usually consist of a confused jumble of colours, rivalling Joseph's coat, or a bottle of mixed pickles, in their picturesque design. There is certainly *an attempt* to give an idea of the "spheres" by blurred, exaggerated, and grotesque reproductions of earthly landscapes; and, in one case, Mr.

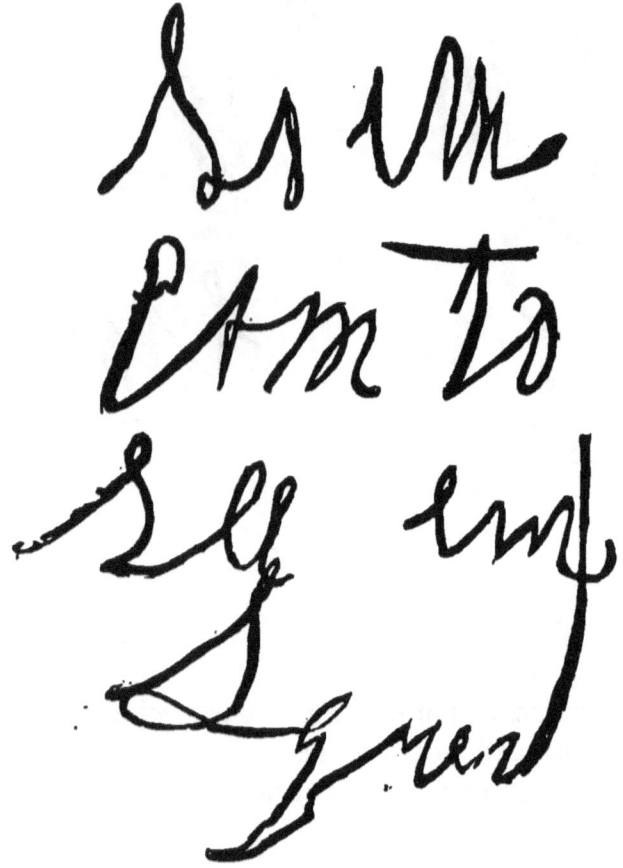

("*So him come to see him, squaw.*" This was addressed to Mrs. Burns.)

David Duguid, "a working cabinet-maker," of Glasgow, "under the guiding influence of Marcus Baker," is said to have given signs of real artistic ability. He "wrought with closed eyes," and appeared so deeply entranced as not to hear persons speak. But though he could not, the spirit could, and replied *through the medium*, in answer to inquiries, that he was not Marcus Baker (what a *shady*, deceitful lot these ghosts must be!) but the spirit of a Dutch painter, born in 1636, and who died in 1681. Subsequently, when the medium had read up a little and fixed upon a name for the spirit, he was declared to be Jacob Ruysdael, and Mr. Duguid reproduced that artist's *chef d'œuvre*, which any one looking at "Cassell's Art Treasures Exhibitor" (page 301) may see engraved. Far be it from me to say that the mediumistic cabinet-maker had ever seen Messrs. Cassell's excellent book!* It was rather casting a slur upon the work of a brother spirit, though, when the medium's "invisible guides" recommended that he should pursue his studies in the Government School of Art; but it is satisfactory that they were justified in giving the ghostly Ruysdael a snub, for the mortals made Duguid do better than he ever did while under spirit training.

HEALING MEDIUMSHIP.

The last Conference of Spiritualists had little of interest in it. One humorous touch was, however, imparted to the proceedings by a remark that Spiritualism had been too much given to cultivating the scientific, instead of seeking to win the poorer classes. This, at a meeting presided over by a scientific ex-lecturer for "Dr." Khan, and a philosophic muffin-man of Liverpool, was sublime!

One of the prominent topics, though, was interesting to the public, as affecting the pockets and the lives of the people. There was a discussion upon the advisability of establishing a Central Spiritual Hospital, where the me-

---

* In a new work, given through the mediumship of the "working cabinet-maker," and entitled "Hafed, Prince of Persia," Messrs. Cassell, Petter, and Galpin have discovered that the pictures in their "Illustrated Bible," many of them by living artists, are pirated and reproduced, "almost line for line," as the work of the spirits!

diumistic "doctors" could always keep in reserve "a strong battery of spiritual power." If possible, also, it was thought better that these spiritual quacks should be "clairvoyants," that they might be able "to see through the patient's body to the seat of the disease."

"We should not be at all astonished," says the "Standard,"* "to learn that some of those clairvoyants, if they tried hard, could see into the middle of next week, but just at the moment they are too busily employed seeing their way into other people's pockets to have leisure for anything else. No site was mentioned for the proposed central hospital; but we trust the suggestion of the neighbourhood of Colney Hatch as extremely eligible, will not be taken as too officious."

But, joking apart, it is wonderful what these disembodied spirits can do through the healers, if we only accept all that is told of them. How diseases, baffling the skill of physicians, are cured by the simple laying-on of hands, may be gathered from Mr. A. C. Burke's † list of Dr. Mack's cures, from which I cull the following:

"No. 20.—Gentleman suffering from the infirmities of old age—*a rather common complaint;* but, really, in the present age of miracles, it seems hard to say what spirit power may not effect, even in the case of such a complaint as this. . . . . No. 23.—Skin disease from birth, age nearly twenty years: had never known, in her own case, what perspiration was, except in the feet and hands. After two or three weeks' treatment the skin had become soft and pleasant, the pores fully opened and relieved, and all roughness and irruption had disappeared. This case—as, indeed, do all the rest—reminds us of the cures wrought

---

* November 5th, 1875.
† This gentleman's wife has a "gift of healing" also.

by Christ, and calls to our mind the poem by N. P. Willis, in which he says:

> 'And lo! the scales fell from him, and his blood
> Coursed with delicious coolness through his veins;
> And his dry palms grew moist, and on his brow
> The dewy softness of an infant stole.'"*

Dr. Newton—from the States, of course!—was a very noted "progressive physician," who "eradicated all forms of disease of recent or long standing, *by the laying-on of hands and* NAZARENE *remedies.*" "It will be new," says the "Daily Telegraph,"† "though possibly not startling, to many persons, to be informed that Dr. Newton considers himself quite on a par with 'the Nazarene,' as he familiarly terms One whom we hesitate to name in such a context. The Nazarene is in the habit of appearing to him frequently, and tells him that the possession of these gifts (of healing) is accorded to him very much because he has not fallen into the mistake of deifying Christ. Such is Dr. Newton's theology — such the profession which develops into his extraordinary *practice*. It will shock many readers, but it is only necessary, in order to show the position assumed by this medium, if we quote his own words on the subject: 'The Nazarene appeared to me and said, "Brother, there's ten thousand spirits brighter and better than me in heaven. If you was to see me among fifty others, you wouldn't know me." Says I, "I think I should; I should know your *beautiful curly hair*." The Nazarene made some noise in Judæa, but nothing like what I'm going to make in London!'

"As he was coming to the Progressive Library that morning, the horse in the hansom cab was taken with the

---

* "Medium and Daybreak," September 10th, 1875.
† June 7th, 1870.

'blind staggers.' 'The people began to make a fuss,' said he, 'but I jumped out, laid my hands on the horse's head, and he was all right in a minute.'"

As Dr. Newton "cured by faith," that horse had blind faith and "blind staggers" also!

The extent of the evil will be seen by a glance at the Spiritualist newspapers, whose columns are half filled with the puffs and advertisements of the "healers." Here we find that " Dr. John Hunter and Dr. Mesmer may be consulted through the mediumship of Mr. Robert Harper," that "Mrs. Empson undertakes the treatment of diseases under the direction of spirit physicians ;" and Mr. and Mrs. E. W. Green give, through "the little spirit 'Snowdrop' and the Indian chief 'Blackhawk,'" their "medical diagnosis by lock of hair."

Miss Lottie Fowler can be consulted "on either medical or business affairs connected with the living and the dead;" and Miss Chandos "undertakes to *eradicate* consumption, cancer, insanity, dipsomania, and all nervous and infantile diseases."

All these people can make the lame to be made whole, the blind to see, and the deaf to hear like the old lady's wonderful ear-trumpet, by aid of which

> "The very next day
> She heard from her husband in Botany Bay."

We have "healing mesmerists" and "medical clairvoyants" as thick as mushrooms after rain, and there are "institutions" of all kinds. One of the Spiritual "doctors," Mr. Coates, who is a "Psychopathic *Institute*" himself, ("I thank thee, *Burns,* for teaching me that word!"*) at

---

* See Mr. Burns for the *singular* meaning of "Institute," Chapter XIII.

Liverpool, near the region of Everton toffee, has thought better of it, and issued

A DISCLAIMER.

To all Spiritualists,—In an ill-advised moment, listening to the suggestions of injudicious friends, I permitted my agent to have the letters " Dr." prefixed to my name on posters, advertisements, &c. At the earliest opportunity I had them struck out, and I beg most respectfully to state that I am not a " Dr." I have no right to the appellation. I regret ever having used it, and however difficult or painful it is to me to make this public retractation, I cannot permit another hour to pass without doing so, as it is a duty I owe to myself, my friends, and the readers of your paper, as well as a rebuke to those who advised in this matter. Permit me to be recognized among you again as yours sincerely, JAMES COATES.*

I am fearful that this *Mr.* Coates must have had more reasons than the pricking of his conscience when he resigned his title, though ! But he has not the strength of mind of some others, who through good report and evil report still stick to their " degree." On this point of the healers I am at one with the Spiritualists—that it demands further investigation. In detail we differ somewhat, as I would require it for these " doctors" at the hands of the Metropolitan Police. I trust we shall soon see the law put in force, and cognizance taken of such as may only be possessed of bogus degrees, if any. Good gracious, what a stampede, what an " awaying" to the " Land of the West" there would be, then!

---

* "Medium and Daybreak," Sept. 17th, 1875.

Of the other phases of mediumship I shall speak at greater length elsewhere when exposing some of the many frauds of the media, but omitting a record of the peccadillos of minor mediums, whose names and whose immoralities are legion. Those who wish to rake up the unsavoury mess need only take a file of American papers, for some very racy, if not proper, reading.

CHAPTER IX.

THE INVASION OF THE MEDIA.

Early Professors — The "great wave" of Spiritualism — The "almighty Dollar"—*Place aux Dames*—Aërial Transition—Illusionists *v.* the Rival "Doctors"—Two of a trade never agree—A Mediumistic Monck—The Black Art in the Isle of Wight—A Travelling Representative—"The Poor Player"—"Washee-washee"—Sad about Mr. Cooper !— Lake Pleasant—" Grotesque *rencontres* "—The People's Garden—A Spirit Navvy—Spiritualism like an Inkstand !—A Testimonial of "Brass ! "— "Airy Daniel" and Dark *Séances*, "Admirable for a flirtation" — Mr. Williams "at home."

UP to the year 1853 England had been singularly and happily free from Spiritualistic taint, but such a prolific gold mine could not long remain unworked.

The invasion of the media commenced with the advent of Mrs. Haydon about this time, she being the first to establish a spirit-rapping store, in Queen Anne Street, and unfold the mysteries of Spiritualism to a public ever ready to pay for novelty. Foster followed with his arm-and-spirit lithography, and, making the "upper ten" curious, managed to reap a rich harvest in London. Then we had another American named Colchester, whose only pretention to being a medium was the fact of his telling a number of names written upon separate slips of paper by various persons—a trick now included in the *rôle* of the ordinary conjuror; Mrs. A. E. Newton, "a medium, a seer, which I take to be a superior development," says our old friend Coleman; and Home came in 1855.

There were others I need not name from the States, and English media were also quickly thrust upon the home market. Still, the greater number even to the present day are of American manufacture. A liberal supply of the article has always been kept up by our Transatlantic brethren, and they kindly send to "Merrie England" the foremost of the mystic fraternity, who, while they raise the spirits of the dead, depress the spirits of the living.

Hither the mediums troop—most to be detected, but all to make money, so a fig for the exposure! We have been overrun with trance and test mediums, inspirationists, rappers, writing, seeing, hearing, healing, and materializing mediums, with all the "properties" of their weird art—the skulls, dark lanterns, guitars, tambourines, and "latest things in ghosts," &c., &c., &c., and in the darkened room the "manifestations" which come in cycles—"in great waves"—are produced *if the circumstances be favourable;* but in any and every case, John Bull is eased of his cash. At length, however, the Bull's eye is upon their doings, which cannot be kept so "dark" as of yore, and their tricks are of little avail. The novelty has worn off; the golden shower has ceased; the Pactolian stream runs dry. So, away! Away with the inspirationists!—the trance, test, rapping, writing, seeing, hearing, healing, and materializing media, with their boxes containing the "trappings and the suits of woe" in which the spirits revisit the earth; all the mystic paraphernalia, even to the "latest thing in ghosts," labelled—"This side up. With care. Not wanted on the voyage;"—for the "great wave" of Spiritualism is ebbing from our English shores, and crossing old Neptune's domains "back again"—(a feat never accomplished successfully by your countrymen, O Burns!) to the Land of the West, where Brother Jonathan is still hungering to be cajoled and thirsting to be cheated —where his purse-strings are still loose, and the life-blood of Spiritualism (the "almighty dollar") rolls merrily about. But, "be in time!" Even here the game will not last for ever! "Make your hay while the sun shines," for ye know not when the vessel of glass may break, and the mediumistic crew be overwhelmed by the "great waves" of a purer faith.

I shall not attempt to enumerate all the media even in London, where we still have them (mostly very small fry, indeed!) east, west, north, and south; but I must name a few, not in the order of their coming, but with the view of introducing some of the more prominent of the medial *dramatis personæ* to the British public.

Place aux dames! The lady formerly known as Miss Nicholls, when Westbourne Grove delighted in her "faces," and now as Mrs. Guppy-Volckman, is certainly the *greatest* personage in the medial world, and one of some weight amongst the Spiritualists. Her first husband, Samuel Guppy, "of Calcutta and Bristol," was the author of a large work, entitled "Mary Jane," attributing the phenomena of Spiritualism to some chemical law; this gentleman died at the ripe age of eighty-four, upon January 18th, 1875, and his widow was led (to the altar I was going to say) to the registrar's office, to enter the bonds of wedlock a second time, upon August 12th in the same year, by Mr. William Volckman — hence the euphonistic name of Guppy-Volckman.

Since 1867 this lady has enjoyed a reputation for producing choice flowers and fruits (all of earthly origin, fresh from Covent Garden) at her *séances*; but the great marvel by which she obtains a niche in the Spiritual Temple of Fame is that she was taken up from her household accounts, *en déshabille*, at Highbury Hill Park, and carried *by the spirits* to 69 Lamb's Conduit Street, where, when she dropped through the roof and through several ceilings (without leaving any apertures), she came down " plump " upon the centre of a table, the ink with which those "household accounts" were being made up still wet in the pen !

> "There is a lady, Mrs. Guppy—
> Mark, shallow scientific puppy !—
> The heaviest she in London, marry,
> Her, spirits three long miles did carry.
>
> Upon a table down they set her,
> Within closed doors. What ! you know better,
> And we 're all dupes and self-deceivers ?
> Yah ! Sadduces and unbelievers ! "*

It seems this "spiritual draw"† took place at Messrs. Herne and Williams's *séance*, about June, 1871. There were present three ladies and eight gentlemen. The doors being locked and the room darkened, one of the circle requested "Katie," in a joking way, to "bring Mrs. G.;" another said, " Good gracious ! I hope not ; she is one of the biggest women in London ;" but "Katie" said, "I will! I will! I will!" and John's rough voice shouted, " You can't do it, Katie." Then says " H. Y.," " a Manchester merchant, of high respectability," in the " Echo," of June 8th, 1871 : " We were all laughing and joking at the absurdity of the idea, when John's voice called out, ' Keep still, can't you?' In an instant somebody called out, ' Good God ! there is something on my head,' simultaneously with a heavy bump on the table and one or two screams. A

---

* "Punch."
† Mrs. Guppy's flight is compared by Fritz ("Where are the Dead?") to the catching away of Philip the Evangelist by the Spirit of the Lord, with the lifting up of Ezekiel, and with the taking up to heaven of Elijah.

match was instantly struck, and there was Mrs. G. standing on the centre of the table, with the whole of us seated round the table, closely packed together, as we sat at the commencement. . . . . Both doors were still locked. Our attention was, however, directed to Mrs. G., who appeared to be in a trance and perfectly motionless. Great fears were entertained that the shock would be injurious to her, supposing it to be really Mrs. G., and not some phantom in her image; but John's voice called out, ' She will soon be all right.' She had one arm over her eyes, with a pen in her hand, and an account-book in her other hand, which was hanging by her side. When she came round, she seemed very much affected, and began to cry. She told us that the last thing she could remember was that she was sitting at home, about three miles away, making up her week's accounts of household expenditure, and that Miss N. was in the room with her reading the paper. The ink in the pen was wet; and the last word she had written,* or rather begun to write, for it was one or two letters short of completion, was smeared and scarcely dry. From the joking remark about bringing Mrs. G., to the time she was on the table, three minutes did not elapse. The possibility of her being concealed in the room is as absurd as the idea of her acting in collusion with the media." "H.Y.," that Manchester merchant "of credit and renown," is welcome to his easy faith; but *I* cannot overlook those two doors from which "attention was, however, directed;" nor do I see in the narrative anything to shake me in my scepticism.

"There is one trifling inconsistency," says the "Quarterly Review," 1871, "we should like explained before we can accept these narratives as veracious. The invisible

---

* Said to be "pickles"!

spirits at Mrs. Guppy's command can obviously do as much for her as did the obedient Jins for the heroes and heroines of the immortal tales that charm the youth of successive generations. If they can bring in any quantity of fruits, flowers, and ices for a dessert, they must surely be able to furnish forth her breakfast and her dinner-tables. When she wishes to travel, they save her not merely the fatigue of the journey, but the cost of cabs and railway fares. What on earth, then, has Mrs. Guppy got to do with 'household accounts'?"

GEORGE SEXTON, "M.A., M.D., LL.D., F.R.G.S., F.Z.S., Honorary Member of L'Accademia dei Quarito at Rome, Honorary Member of the American Anthropological Association, &c., &c., &c.," is believed to have commenced life as a palliasse-maker. Before the Doctor joined the "new religion" as a "Christian Spiritualist," he had been "connected with the free-thought movement for twenty years,"* also engaged as lecturer for that German barber and disgusting quack, "Dr." Khan, at his notorious museum in Tichborne Street; now happily extinguished.

In "Revelations of Quacks and Quackery," by F. B. Courtenay, Member of the Royal College of Surgeons,† we read a few revelations concerning Khan's Museum, and "Christopher Crushgammon, Esq., M.D.," which should be of interest to "Christian" and other Spiritualists. Well, Dr. Sexton, who commenced his career of talkist as a missionary and blossomed into a Spiritualist lecturer, is now a leader of the Christians in that sect, and the only man to be found at the Liverpool Conference of the *National Association*, 1873, to say a word for the Bible, which he declared "might be accepted in its entirety;" and, after that,

---

* "The Spiritualist," April 1st, 1873.
† London: Baillière, Tyndall, and Cox, Medical Publishers.—Page 95.

surely none could doubt! Nevertheless, it seems that Christianity is at a discount amongst the Pantheon's devotees; and the editor, Dr. Sexton, in the "Christian Spiritualist" for September 1st, 1875, announced the discontinuance of that journal "on account of the scanty support afforded it by those whose principles it was intended specially to set forth, and to which it has been conscientiously devoted."

And, if we are to believe Mr. F. R. Young (Sexton's predecessor in the editorial chair), the pugnacious Doctor is a martyr for his new faith.

Mr. Young writes:

"You may be an atheist, a pantheist, a deist, or almost anything you like, and your theological opinions will not be used to your disadvantage; but if you are so unfortunate as to be a Christian, and say so, if you tell the Spiritualist body that you believe in Jesus Christ as the Lord of your life, and the Teacher from whose verdict there lies, and can lie, no right of appeal, it is true you are not excommunicated—the fact that you are a Spiritualist is still admitted; but you are looked upon with eyes more or less unfriendly, and a wonder is expressed how, believing in Spiritualism, you can at the same time be a Christian."

For a time—a very short time—the doctor ventured out to prove the truth of Spiritualism (or to obtain a livelihood) by reproducing some of my illusions, with, as he said in his advertisement, "machinery especially made for the purpose." In truth, he bought some old and worn-out rubbish that had been used by a daughter of the late Professor Anderson, "Wizard of the North," and failed ignominiously after a very short career.

The joke is that none of the tricks attempted to be imitated by this would-be exposer had any reference to Spiritualism whatever; and when Dr. Monck appeared upon the scene as another imitator of the illusionists, there were too many Richards in the field, and they set to and devoured each other, like the Kilkenny cats. "Just now," says Mr. Hinde, in "Bell's Weekly Messenger," "there is a serious split in the Spiritualistic camp, or perhaps it would be a more appropriate expression to say, that the breach which has so long divided the leading Spiritualists has been very greatly widened by the paper war in which Dr. Sexton and Dr. Monck have recently indulged, and which, while it may have been very edifying to the true believers, and received by them as another proof of the purity, goodness, holiness, and truthfulness of the religion they profess to believe, has had the effect of diverting the outside public, and filling the Egyptian Hall to overflowing. A writer in 'Human Nature' has cognomenized Dr. Sexton as 'an avenging spirit,' in so far as his alleged exposure of Maskelyne and Cooke is concerned. It unfortunately happens, as appears from the Spiritualistic publications, that Dr. Monck has also started 'on his own hook' in the exposure and avenging line. This proceeding has, not unnaturally, given great umbrage to Dr. Sexton, 'the original avenger,' who complains that it is rather hard, after he has expended so much time and money in the matter, that he should be completely *supplanted* in his public work by another man, who is indebted to Dr. Sexton for all he knows on the subject. To this charge Dr. Monck gives a flat denial, and, in doing so, he administers a little wholesome correction to his brother avenger, by informing him that if the interests of Spiritualism (*private* interests being put on one side) rendered it necessary that Dr. Sexton should expose the conjurors, it is surely needful that other lecturers should stand up in the defence of Spiritualism now that the jugglers have increased their numbers, according to Dr. Sexton, by 'a dozen or more.' Avenger *secundus* adds the significant remark, which the public will doubtless at once see the full force of and estimate at its proper value, while the illusionists will no doubt laugh most consummately thereat—he says, 'the field is ample enough to employ another score of *exposé* lecturers without necessarily creating an ill feeling among them.' A greater compliment to the skill of the conjurors, and a more humiliating confession of the weakness and absurdity of Spiritualism, it would be impossible for any one to make."

Dr. MONCK—who has shot like a meteor over the Spiritualistic sky—is, or was, a Unitarian minister of Bristol. Now, the Monck—naturally taking precedence of the Sexton—has been eagerly watched by the Spiritualist stargazers, while his adversary is, in sporting parlance, "nowhere!"—and this is the story which gained him admittance to that "inner circle" of the "Pantheon," where the chief occupations of life seem to be conducted in outer darkness.

At Bristol, in the midsummer of 1871, about half-past one o'clock in the morning, Dr. Monck was suddenly missed from his bed by a Mr. Rowland, who seems to have shared its accommodation with him; and the anything but ascetic Monck found himself at an hotel at Swindon—distant forty-two miles—without his hat, coat, or waistcoat, half an hour afterwards. As the gentleman had those nether garments on which it is not proper to name to ears polite,* we may assume he went to bed as the song says "My son John" did;† and if so, would it

---

* Moral America veils the nakedness of its table and chair-legs with the same articles of attire!

"Where the legs of the tables in tr——s are dressed,
Away, far away, to the Land of the West."

† "My son John
Went to bed with his tr——s on."
—*Old Song.*

be proper to ask why he did not do the "usual" in doffing those garments? Had he been dining out, or what?

We have a story of the worthy minister's doings in the Isle of Wight, which might fairly be put down to the power of *spirits* by the most sceptical person.

The doctor had gone on the coach for a trip to Carisbrooke, and on arriving at that place the passengers dined together, and a merry party there was! "Dinner over, the table was covered, and wine-glasses and bottles crowned the festive board. The glasses were filled all round.

"Now was 'Samuel's'* opportunity, and a vigorous use he made of it; for he tumbled glass after glass on the table, spilling the wine, and exasperating the would-be imbibers. It was really amusing to see a thirsty soul, with the pleasure begotten of anticipation smiling in his face, stretch out his hand to lift the tempting glass, and then to behold his rueful expression of countenance as, like Tantalus of old, he saw the vinous receptacle recede from him, lean gracefully at an angle of forty-five degrees, and then pour out his coveted wine—an oblation to no better god than the table-cloth.

"But one *bon-vivant* was treated to a still greater surprise, for just as he was about to take his brimming glass, the wine obligingly ejected itself on his knees, and then performing a masterly somersault, stood on its mouth bottom upwards."†

The "spirits" must have got into the heads of some, at least, of this jovial crew by the coach to Carisbrooke! Dr. Monck has also been "Hoisted up into the air" (in the darkness) "from nine to eighteen inches, according to the resistant nature of the temperament of those persons who held his feet; and Mr. Burns was then told to stand in

---

* Dr. Morck's "spirit guide."   † "The Medium," November 5th, 1875.

front of Dr. Monck. He did so, supporting his hands on a chair which stood before him. The spirit said he would place Dr. Monck on his shoulders. Soon the voice of the doctor was heard up in the air, and his feet pawed at Mr. Burns's back, but the spirit complained that he could not place the medium on Mr. Burns's shoulders. Another effort was made, and Dr. Monck was gently seated on Mr. Burns's neck, with the doctor's legs down his breast. The spirit called for a light, that the company might 'see a parson ride on Jamie Burns's shoulders.' A match was struck, extinguished after a few moments, and the entranced medium was lifted down from his seat as gently as he was placed there."* This is a terribly confused account, and evidently written in a mental fog. Are we to take it that the doctor's legs were down his own breast, or what? Oh, those powerful *spirits!* Dr. Monck has also been levited "on to the shoulders of a lady "† (who must be not only strong-minded but strong-backed), and has given that shallow trick of the "direct spirit voice, whilst the medium's mouth is filled with water;" which, as anybody but a Spiritualist must see, is accomplished by the medium swallowing the water before speaking, and re-filling the mouth from a secreted bottle containing *aqua pura* afterwards!

Dr. Monck has several "controls;" one, "the Rev. Mr. So-and-So, a minister of the Church of England, who delivered a most laughable burlesque on the mannerisms, slang, and set phrases of the present fashionable mode of preaching, thoroughly ignoring that deformity known as the letter R;" ‡ and a lady spirit, addicted to the peculiarly unlady-like habit of putting her feet upon the table.

---

* "The Medium," March 12th, 1875.
† "The Spiritualist," October 1st, 1875.
‡ "The Spiritualist," October 1st, 1875.

By the aid of his principal spirit guide, "Samuel, formerly a shipwright in Portsmouth Dockyard," Dr. Monck "elongates" to any extent, which can scarcely be wondered at, when we know how the media do go in for stretching —the truth especially!

It is not worth while giving more of the marvels of this professor of legerdemain. The London public at least are pretty well posted up in them, and at the Egyptian Hall can see the luminous hands, the musical box which stops at command—ay, "at half a note," like Dr. Monck's; and all and sundry of the effects produced by the Bristol minister who "rows"—nay, nearly fights—in the same boat with Sexton.

Mr. JAMES J. MORSE—formerly barman, and still connected with the spirits, though an I.O.G.T.,* and late with Mr. Burns, (of) the Spiritual Institution, as assistant—is now an Inspirational Trance Speaker, and "very like a whale" amongst the minnows in the shallow waters of Spiritualism. His chief controls are "a strolling player;" Mr. Walter Arthur Clegg, a rheumaticky old man, "a carter in earth-life;" and "Tien-sien-tie," a genuine "Washee-washee" and "Mandarin of the Second Order," who was attached to his pigtail like an English Jack Tar of the Pre-Ironclad Period,—with a difference!—at Pekin about a century and a quarter back.

Mr. Morse has had a twelve months' run through "the States," and has detailed his experiences there for the benefit of the poor moths who fluttered round the Spiritual rushlight at the Conference of the National Association,

---

* Which, by dint of perseverance, I have discovered to mean—"Order of Good Templars." It has been suggested that "I" stands for "Independent," but I should say it means "initiate"—he having been called *from* the Bar so recently.

held in November, 1875, in the now-hallowed precincts of Bloomsbury. He had visited New Haven, Connecticut—the "City of Elms," in the "Wooden Nutmeg State;"—and at Boston, the Hub of the Universe, he met Mr. J. B. Rich, "a smart man," who presides over the business department of the "Banner of Light," and Mr. Luther Colby, its editor. Mr. Morse "orated" for the Music Hall Society. He says:

"Spiritualism is decidedly a recognized fact in Boston. The press give it respectful notice, while the pulpit contents itself with an occasional grumble. On the houses in many of the streets, notably the most prominent ones, Washington Street, Tremont Street, and Shawmut Avenue, the signs of test mediums, clairvoyants, and magnetic healers are quite numerous, while their advertisements are to be found in several daily papers." And, if the English people would only consent, we might have all this here! At Philadelphia he met Dr. H. T. Child, the president of the local Spiritual Society—an office he has resigned (?) since "sweet Katey King's" exposure; and Mr. Morse, in consequence of the hubbub caused by this "imbroglio," found his position "rendered anything but enviable" in "the Quaker city—the home of the Pilgrim Fathers."

He attended several *séances;* at one of these, he says, "Quite a quantity of flowers and ferns, with some fruit, was brought, and Mr. Cooper, this time, also received a white pigeon. I regret to say that a gentleman of the canine persuasion subsequently made a breakfast of them both."* Poor Mr. Cooper! But I have long thought that spiritualists were "going to the dogs" rapidly. Mr. Morse does not accept all he has heard in America; indeed, he considers some of the schemes broached there in connection

---

* "The Spiritualist," November 5th, 1875.

with the faith "wild." Perhaps his happiest experiences in that land of "ingrained speculators" was at the annual camp meeting of the Lake Pleasant Spiritualists' Association, opened on Sunday, August 8th, 1875, at Montague, Massachusetts, some one hundred miles from Boston, whence excursion tickets were issued by the railway companies. Here,—what with skiffs upon the lake, bath-houses for ladies and gentlemen, and shady walks "for meditative students and—lovers!"—spiritualists *and others* found many attractions. The "spiritual" nature of the meeting seems to have been strangely ignored. "One event of an unique nature" which Mr. Morse notices, may serve to bring this out more fully: "This was what is known as a 'sheet and pillow-case' or 'phantom party.' The participants are draped in sheets, turbaned with pillow-cases, and adorned with natural flowers, while some provide dresses similar to those worn by the *Follies* during carnival times. For the first hour and a half all are masked, and the complete change the dress makes in one's appearance, and the fact *that many gentlemen robe as ladies*, leads to some comical and grotesque *rencontres*."* So, while we poor insulated and old-world people take even our amusements gravely, the ghost-ridden people of Boston, U.S.A., shake a very loose leg indeed at a spiritualist camp meeting. Skating rinks are all very well, and spelling "bees" may be endured; but pray do not introduce "phantom parties" into England, if you please, Brother Jonathan!

But the English "faithful" enjoy themselves in a strange manner sometimes, especially when they repair for a day's pleasure to the People's Garden, Willesden, and have merry-go-rounds, dancing on the "largest platform in the

---

* "The Spiritualist," October 8th, 1875.

world," and donkey races, *not* by members of the National Ass-ociation!

Before passing from the fascinating trance-speaker, Mr. Morse, I must perforce mention his appearance and "oratory," which, though not supposed to give any signs of book knowledge, is said to owe a good deal to Combe's "Science and Religion."

The Travelling Representative of the Spiritual Institution—(what that means "nobody tells—'cause nobody knows!")—is described as looking "more like a very respectable undertaker's assistant than anything else."* His "control," "Tien-sien-tie," declares he has seen "the individual called Jesus of Nazareth in the spirit world, and did not consider Him more divine in His origin than other spirits in His own sphere, which, however, was an advanced one."†

Mr. Morse's spirit navvy speaks of "them shivery-shaky kind o' people called 'mediums,'" and declares he finds it easier to go "slantindicular," than straight to a place; and his "strolling player," "in his customary humorous style," sometimes makes "many good points by comparing Spiritualism to an inkstand"! ‡

Of Mr. CHARLES E. WILLIAMS (late of Herne and Williams) it will be enough to say that he is great at "materialization" *in the dark*. Certainly this style of *séance* is considered objectionable even by some Spiritualists. "Airy Daniel," who was not above doing a little with "lights down" himself once, remarks that "dark sittings are most fearful stumbling-blocks in the way of anything like scientific investigation. One fact given in

---

* "Daily Telegraph," March 10th, 1870.
† " The Spiritualist," May 22nd, 1874.
‡ " Medium and Daybreak," November 12th, 1875.

the light, no matter how trifling it may seem, constitutes an incontrovertible truth; whereas, where there is darkness, it paves the way to suspicion, to say the least of it."* But one fact remains: *dark séances pay*. The Spiritualist and the unbeliever alike favour what a reverend gentleman, well posted-up in such (Spiritualistic) matters, declares to be a mistake for test purposes, but "admirable for a flirtation."

Through the kindness of my friend, Mr. John Algernon Clarke, I am enabled to give "a faithful report" of one of Mr. Williams's *séances*. This was held in rooms over a tailor's shop at 61 Lamb's Conduit Street, near the Foundling Hospital. There was much chattering and merriment, the usual and suspicious re-arrangement of the circle, so that the known and trusted faithful should close round and act as a bodyguard to the "medium," and the inevitable long waits—badly filled in by tuneless singing to "harmonize the influences."

When the "manifestations" did come, they were "of the most stupid and non-angelic character," until *the* "features" of the evening, "John King" and "Peter," put in an appearance. "Some of the sitters," says Mr. Clarke, "rather too hurriedly, I thought, recognized the presence of 'John King.' After a few gleams, gathering in brightness, I perceived a white turban and something like a long black beard, with the shoulders and breast part of a white robe. Evidently here was a figure of a man, life size, flitting a little to the right or left, and up and down, and suddenly showing just the face and little else, for a moment or two only in each position. This gave the impression that a self-luminous spirit was floating about the space just in front of the cabinet. I could see that the source of

---

* "Medium and Daybreak," October 15th, 1875.

the faint light was in the hands of the spirit form. Some of the sitters asked John to let them hold his lamp. I don't know whether he parted with it; but I was told that he sometimes does, and that it is in shape and size somewhat like a cake of soap. I believe that the light can be exactly imitated by an electrical apparatus, and that phosphorus and oil will also give a similar light, and will burn for a few seconds, even in a close-stopped bottle. The gruff low voice of 'John King' was precisely what I should expect to hear if Mr. Williams were to try and imitate it through a paper cone. The feminine nasal weak little voice of 'Peter' is precisely what I should expect to hear if Mr. Williams were to try and imitate it in falsetto. In appearance 'Peter' was 'John King' with his beard off. What impressed me most forcibly, were these observations which I made: the spirit of 'John King' had on his face an exact facsimile of Mr. Williams's peculiar and unmistakable nose. This I am confident about, though the figure kept moving and showing itself only by fitful flashes, without ever confronting us and remaining for our deliberate examination. When John King's head was seen near to the ceiling, immediately over the centre of the table, it was about the same elevation as Mr. Williams's head would be if he stood upon the table: I crossed one of my legs over the other, so as to press one knee against the under side of the table-top, and I distinctly felt just a slight depression of the table and its rise again when the figure of John King came above the table and went off again. I could not feel for myself whether it were a man or not, because the young lady next me held my hand (on that side) extra hard when the figure came near us. This was the same lady who sat next the medium during the first series of manifestations. Anybody could have stepped from the cabinet on to the table; and at the end of the *séance* I made this observation: the table (a handsome one) was constructed with a centre pedestal, and feet projecting so far outward that the weight of a man upon the table, even near the edge of the top, would not be liable to tilt it; and further, there were upright struts or pillars supporting the table-top, within a short distance of the edge, so that when I pressed downwards upon one edge of the table, it did not bend or creak. If a man were walking about on it, I am satisfied that any depression on one side or the other would be only just perceptible, as in the experiment which I tried with my knee.

"One theory accounting for this manifestation, is that the forms we saw were living spirits materialized for the time being, and able to move and talk. Nobody can prove it was so. My theory is that Mr. Williams dressed up and personified John King and Peter. Nobody can prove that it wasn't so.

"I neither saw, heard, nor otherwise perceived by any of my senses anything supernatural, unless my theory is to be rejected, and the Spiritualist theory held to be the more probable of the two. But I lost my five shillings, which fee was paid to Mr. Williams at the bottom of the stairs as we left the place.

"I fancy that some other people present got more fun for their money. There was a good deal of tittering from some parts of the circle; and in the last *séance*, a very amused-looking young gentleman stood behind the brisk young damsel who sat next me. Leaning a little in that direction, I could tell by the whispering, and the breaths, and the giggling, that their faces had been very much brought together. I heard her whisper (not at all cross, I assure you), 'If you don't behave, you shan't come to a *séance* with me any more;' and after more wriggling and giggling, 'If you do that again I shall bite you.'"

CHAPTER X.

A FEW EXPOSURES.

Gentle Showers—"Lost Lenore"—Sugar-candy—Spirits Moulting!—Miss S.'s *chignon*—A Poet "King"—An "Indescribable" Being described—"Sweet William, the Carpenter"—The Mysteries of a Dark *Séance*—A little Blonde's taper Digits—A "Seeing" Medium—"Sweet William" finds a Rival Carpenter—"The RING of all the best Mediums!"—Bastian and Taylor—My Grandmother!—A lucid Description—A Holland's Gin (Trap)—Investigating "Blackguards"—"Foregone Conclusions and Ignorance"—Spirit Photos—Ghosts *ad lib*. "Come like Shadows"—Double *Exposures*—A *Trial* for the Photographers—Butter-cloth Egerton—"Jack Tod," the Liverpool Spirit—Virtue and "Vice" go hand in hand—Serious Thoughts.

MISS SHOWERS has, or had, for familiar spirits, I believe, "Peter," a disreputable market gardener, who sings, or sang, in a baritone voice, "Listen to the Whip-poor-Will a-singin' on a tree," and "Florence Maple," a spirit who gave a wrong address in Aberdeen as her abode in earth-life. I know "Lenore Fitzwarren" is one of this lady's "guides," for does not Sir Charles Isham, Bart., vouch for the truth of it, and has he not received a letter in the direct spirit writing from "Lenore"? Sir Charles is never tired of singing the praises of "the lost Lenore," though "it would require a pen far more graphic" than his, he says, "to describe the charming and winning ways of this playful little spirit."

At the house of Mrs. Mackdougal Gregory the spirits find a very hospitable reception, and here it is that "Lenore" has frequently enchanted "dear Sir Charles." "Upon one occasion," says this patient investigator, "I took an impression of her hand and left foot in dough; this I found much better than clay, which I used on former occasions. She allowed me to examine and touch her right foot, both above and below; it was very narrow, and had but two toes. She objected to an impression being taken of it, although I did my best to obtain one; but I hope to be more fortunate on some future occasion." .... "We gave her a small piece of sugar-candy, which I brought for the purpose, requesting her to crush it. She said, 'I must materialize a tooth for that;' and retired behind the curtain. 'Peter' now became witty (!), and, as if assisting in the operation, was heard to exclaim during the process, 'But you don't want a wise tooth.' She soon returned, and another piece of candy being given, she gave unmistakable demonstration of the crushing powers of her teeth."

Now, it seems this investigator had been rewarded by "Lenore's" confidence, inasmuch as she had entered into a correspondence with Sir Charles. There was some little difficulty in doing this, as the "playful little spirit," having "rummaged" Miss Showers' desk overmuch, that young lady had declined to allow her to take such liberties in future, so the aërial being was disconsolate, not having paper to write upon. This want the baronet kindly supplied, sending "Lenore" a writing-desk; paper stamped in colours, with her monogram "L.F.;" and postage stamps.

I cannot but think it unkind of the spirit to use these latter, when the ghostly "Miss Fitzwarren" could so easily have slipped into the worthy baronet's letter-box and deposited her pretty little notes—the monogram stamped in colours—herself. Might not the spirit do so much, and give the penny saved (which is the penny gained) to the Spiritual Institution?

In this case "Lenore" seems to have been much impressed with the kindness of this "B. of B.K."—as the *reduced* "nobleman" at Dartmoor has it—and Sir Charles received several letters, one of which, being a really unique specimen of spirit composition, I must find space for:

"My Dear Sir Charles,—What must you think of me? I am really almost afraid to write to you now, fearing that you will be too angry to take any notice of my letter. However, I must find consolation in the motto—'Better late than never,' and can only hope that you will agree with me there. Rosey has been living very quietly of late, seldom giving any *séances;* in fact, I have almost forgotten the way to materialize, 't is such an age since I last had a try at it.

"I am now residing in Jupiter, and am very happy, though thoroughly under the dominion of 'King Saul,' who is the ruling power there. He is teaching me to fly gracefully, and says I am not a very troublesome pupil, except that I drop my feathers about, and that is, of course, disagreeable. I have a flower undergoing the process of materialization for you, and will enclose it in this letter if it is solid enough to stand the journey through the post. With love from 'Peter' and myself, believe me, dear Sir Charles, yours affectionately,

"Lenore Fitzwarren."*

Miss Showers being musical, of course her spirits are the same, and we have pianoforte performances and singing, interspersed with such edifying information from the

---

* "Medium and Daybreak," August 6th, 1875.

spirits as "prayer gains us salvation. It enables us to get to the top of the tree and sit there," then, after a pause—"but we must not have too many up, or it will break down!"*

Unfortunately Miss Showers was discovered in something very like trickery. The young lady and her mamma were invited to the country house of Serjeant Cox, where "a cabinet was extemporized in the bay of the window," says the Rev. C. Maurice Davies, "over which the curtains were drawn and a shawl pinned. With a confidence which is really charming to contemplate, no 'tests' were asked of the medium—no 'conditions' imposed on the sitters. Miss S. was put in the cabinet with only a chair, and the expectant circle waited with patience. In due time the curtains were drawn aside, and the spirit face appeared at the opening. It was still a facsimile of Miss S., with the eyes piously turned up and a ghostly head-dress covering the hair. One by one the assembled were summoned to look more closely. The initiated gazed and passed on—knowing they must not peep; but alas! one lady who was *not* initiated, and therefore unaware of the tacitly imposed conditions, imitated the example of mother Eve—drew the curtains, and exposed the unspiritual form of Miss S. standing on the chair!—the 'spirit hands' at the same time struggling so convulsively to close the aperture, that the head-gear fell off, and betrayed the somewhat voluminous *chignon* of Miss S. herself! Hereupon ensued a row, it being declared that the medium was killed, though eventually order was restored by the rather incongruous process of a gentleman present singing a comic song. The learned Serjeant still clings to the belief that Miss S. was in a state of 'unconscious somnambulism.' I only hope, if ever I am

---

* Sir Charles Isham, Bart.

arraigned before him in his judicial capacity, he will extend his benevolent credulity to me in an equal degree, and give me the benefit of the doubt."*

Miss Showers must feel that "materialization" is a risky game, so I am happy to find her cultivating the acquaintance of a poetic spirit, "John King," who does *not* "materialize;"—indeed, he gives very sensible advice when he requests Mrs. Showers to "send away the chief spirit" who produces the manifestations.† Time she did, indeed, when the "chief spirit" treats the young lady medium so disgracefully!

But for the spirit poetry. John King (the poet, not the Buccaneer) asks—

> "Have you not seen the swift-running tide
> Bending with violence the firm gutter-side?"‡

To which I can honestly answer that this is one of the phenomena I have *not* observed.

But the poet is not to have all the questions to himself, for Mrs. Frederica Showers inquires, "John, is your name really King?" and "John," through the medium, replies:

> "Yes, King is my name, and with kingly power
> Will I watch by thy side through the dreariest hour."

And then Mrs. Showers proceeds to "draw out" the opinions of the spirit:

"MRS. S. Do you know anything about the devil? Can you tell me about my son?

(Rather an odd mixture, here; eh?)

"'JOHN.'
> In a bright star, ah me, how fair!
> Thy son with God doth dwell;
> He bids me watch o'er thee with care,
> And knows thou farest well."

---

* "Mystic London." Tinsley Brothers.
† "The Spiritualist," October 22nd, 1875.
‡ "The Spiritualist," December 18th, 1874.

(You see, "John" is too 'cute to answer the first part of this question: he will not tell what he knows of the "gentleman in black.")

"MRS. S. Is he happy?" (This of her son.)
"'JOHN.'
> Happy! In that hallowed spot
> Can he be otherwise?
> Wilt thou not pray to share his lot?
> Is it not Paradise?

"MRS. S. Will you ever bring him as you promised?
"'JOHN.'
> Ask not, for time alone will show
> That which, just now, thou mayest not know."*

Doubtless the spirit Pegasus requires a spur; but the lines here are not so lame and halting as some we have seen.† Who knows, if such improvement goes on, but we may have a ghostly Laureate before long?

MISS ANNIE EVA FAY, or MRS. FAY, the celebrated physical and mental test medium, of Louisville, Kentucky"—also known as the "Indescribable Phenomenon"—after "a tour through the principal cities and towns of the States," came to London to startle us with some of the shallowest tricks ever foisted upon the public as "Spiritualism." Her performances at the Hanover Square Rooms having been public, many of my readers will have had an opportunity of judging of the wonders worked by the "Indescribable" one. Mr. Henry Fay, who acted as *séance* director, and whose "lecture" will never be forgotten by those who heard it, whilst not disclaiming supernatural assistance for his wife, was careful in leaving the audience to arrive at their own conclusions upon that point, though amongst Spiritualists she was looked upon as a

---
* "The Spiritualist," October 22nd, 1875.
† See poetic effusions of the spirits, Chapter VII.

medium, and, indeed, asserted that position herself in private always. Her "familiar" was "Sweet William, a carpenter," and that there should be no doubt about his *bonâ fides*, he was made to drive a nail into a piece of wood at one part of the "entertainment," which must have been proof positive to every Spiritualist present!

At the same time that these manifestations were running at the Queen's Concert Rooms, my colleague, Mr. Cooke, was giving an exact re-production of all Miss Fay's tricks in the light *séance*, to the most minute particulars, twice daily at the Egyptian Hall, where I had the pleasure of *explaining* the *modus operandi* of accomplishing the "marvels" of the dark *séance*, which were too simple and absurd to bear any other treatment. Thus was the spirit-work accomplished for "Miss Fay": Some fifteen persons from the audience sat in a circle round the "medium," her husband, the "Colonel," being one. The little blonde then commenced to clap her hands with steady, rhythmical beat, and when the darkness was made "visible," still the clapping continued, while—wonderful to relate!—instruments which had been laid upon the knees of the "sitters" were played upon, &c., &c., that is, the guitar was strummed in the air, bells were rung, knees pinched, whiskers tugged, old fogies chucked under the chin by, oh! such nice little hands!—and the other interesting work of the spirits at *séances* was gone through. Now, all this while the "Colonel" was in the circle, and granted that the persons to his right and left were careful never to let go his hands for a moment, and then unknowingly be both holding his *left hand only*, he could do little to assist his interesting spouse; and she, still clapping those dainty little palms, could, of course, do nothing herself, unless, as soon as the lights were extinguished, she was to change her tactics, and beat—not her hands together—but one hand upon her forehead, or arm, or any exposed part of her body, *which would produce exactly the same sounds as the clapping of the palms*, and leave the taper digits of one hand free to "manifest" upon the Instruments, knees, chins, &c. But, oh dear, no! To show the impossibility of such a thing, one gentleman shall now be allowed to hold the medium's hands;—still a bell shall ring, a guitar be strummed, and possibly the gentleman holding the fair one shall have his face fanned. How, then, can all this be accomplished? Simply thus: "Miss Fay" will pass a bell to the "Colonel's" mouth, which he will shake as a terrier does a rat, the while his boot operates upon the guitar-strings and produces the thrumming; and the medium, with a fan held between her teeth, will gently wave it in the face of him who holds her hand. And this is all that happened in the darkness, and this is what scientific Mr. Crookes declared was "wonderful!" and what Mrs. Burns, who is a "seeing medium," saw several spirits performing for "Miss Fay."

Miss Fay has gone across the "sad sea waves" again to the "land of the West," and, presuming upon the F.R.S.'s recommendation, "announces herself in Boston as 'endorsed by the Royal Society of England.'"

Before I quit the subject I must name how Miss Fay's business agent made an offer to me, by letters which I have now in my possession, that for a sum of money the medium should expose the whole affair, "scientific tests" and all, as she was not properly supported by the Spiritualists; *complicating*, as he says—I suppose he means *implicating*—"at least six *big guns*, the F.R.S. people,"* and "Miss Fay is now every night *materializing and is immence* another point I will give she is in the RING of all

---

* Letter dated "Birmingham, May 12th, 1875."

the best mediums in London and get letters every day that will be big to work upon."* Again, " Some of the parteys that I named in my last to you are trying to persuade Miss Fay to go to *America*, and I am getin tired of *messing* about in this way, and *have fully* made up my mind if she go wich I shall know in a day or two, to *make some* money out of my past *year expierance* and *knowledge* as in a word I have another prety lady that I can bring out, *and* if I *personely can will use all names* and show the whole thing up being the introducer of it in London."†

The managerial offer was not accepted by me, nor did he go to America. He brought out the "prety lady," though, who performed exactly the same tricks as her cousin, "Miss" Fay, and the "Indescribable Phenomenon" took herself off to "the States," where Mrs. Carpenter (Sweet William's rival) is showing up the phenomenal tricks to such an extent that the little blonde latterly has had very meagre audiences, to charm with her grace or astonish by her occult power.

HARRY BASTIAN and MALCOLM TAYLOR were wont to do their spiriting gently in the first storey of a house not far from that abode of many stories, good, bad, and indifferent —the British Museum. Mr. John Algernon Clarke, who attended one of their *séances*, writes:

" Mr. Bastian I found to be a dreamy innocent-looking gentleman, and Mr. Taylor not so. Mr. Bastian did most of the abstracted demeanour, *spirituelle* expression, and lackadaisical sighing. Mr. Taylor did most of the patter, the conversing in Spiritualistic cant about spheres and spirit life, and also started the hymn-singing."

I hope Mr. Clarke found it better than one described by Mr. W. H. Harrison, where the light was so low that he

---

* Letter dated " Birmingham, May 15th, 1875."
† Letter dated " Malvern, May 24th, 1875."

thought he saw a part of* a nose, but was not quite sure upon the point! However, a young lady at the same *séance* saw her grandmother, whom she seems to have recognized more by her gold spectacles than anything else, and a gentleman who writes a London Letter for the "Leamington Chronicle" was enabled to give this lucid account of the old lady: It was a semi-transparent figure, and "you could see the black band and the indistinct white cap, and an inferation of an intimation of an indication of a form, as the outlined transciency of an invisible cloud"!

Messrs. Bastian and Taylor did not altogether satisfy the "Spiritualist" newspaper; indeed, Mr. Harrison declared their dark *séance*, with the mediums tied to a bed-post, to be, at least, open to suspicion.

In Holland they were more than suspected, as will be seen from the following statement, translated from the "Arnheim News" (Dec. 16th, 1874):

"Yesterday evening we were present at a *séance*, at which Messrs. Bastian and Taylor were to show us the 'spirits.' The guests were thirteen in number, besides the 'mental clairvoyant medium,' who formed the company into a circle, and the 'physical medium,' who sat on a chair in the middle. The 'spirits' did their usual work: we felt hand-touches; there was talking through a trumpet; a spring puppet came down upon our knees; above all, 'Johnny' and 'Georgy' (so were our spirits called) played to us delightfully on the guitar. In the midst of all this, Mr. Taylor, who did nothing but tell us he saw spirits, and was held fast by the wrists, passed something he held in his hands to Mr. Bastian. At a given moment, while the guitar was heard thrumming over our heads, at a signal from one of us, a galvanic stream was sent from an adjoining room,

---

* "Spiritualist," May 7th, 1875.

along a platinum wire in the room where we were sitting, and igniting some cotton wool soaked in petroleum in which camphor had been dissolved, gave out a flame which lighted up the apartment. All this was the work of a quarter of a second at most; and what say the undersigned? The 'physical medium,' who was clapping his hands, and was sitting on the extreme edge of his chair, raised the guitar in his right hand, and let the instrument fall before our eyes on the head of one of us, while he gazed with terror and evident anxiety at the flame which had brought everything to light. The mental medium' could not utter a word: he looked annoyed, and muttered something about *blackguards*. Of the undersigned, the five first were aware of the moment at which the guitar fell from the hands of the supposed spirit; the others, that he withdrew his outstretched hand and evinced great anxiety, which possibly explains the fact of his holding the clappers in his hands. One of us put the question to Bastian, whether those present had a right to acknowledge what they had seen with their own eyes: the medium was silent. In another moment the mediums had disappeared: their farewell was, that 'they wished the head of the gentleman on which the instrument fell (who was only slightly hurt) *had been split.*' We inform you of these strange things for the benefit of those who believe in the spiritism of *these* gentlemen.

"We offer our thanks to Mr. Lincker, Secretary of the High Middle-Class School, for the patience with which he waited from eight to half-past nine o'clock for the signal from the first of the undersigned.

"J. TH. CATTIE, "H. H. VAN CAPPELLE,
"I. L. A. J. SPRENGER, "Z. VAN DER VEGTE,
"J. J. WILDSCHUT, "Dr. J. H. ZILVER RUPE,
"J. C. H. HELDRING, "H. PRINS,
"J. F. VAN MANEN."

There must be some answer to such a statement; and what, think you, is it? This: "The trumpery charge" is ascribed to "foregone conclusions and ignorance of psychological phenomena"; and Mr. Harrison, after "examining the facts by the light of experience," "heartily endorses" this view of the matter.*

SPIRIT "PHOTOS."

The first "spirit photographs" obtained in England were either by Mr. F. Parkes at his "sittings à la séance," or Mr. Fred. A. Hudson—*which* is immaterial. The latter gentleman soon got, and still remains, under a cloud, even with Spiritualists themselves, as experts detected unquestionable signs of "double exposure"—a trick by which any photographer can produce "ghosts" *ad libitum*. These spirit figures appeared behind the sitters in the picture; but Holloway rejoices no longer in their presence, and Notting Hill has only plain "Mr. Hudson, Photographer," which is but the shadow of what the great man was.

The late Mr. Samuel Guppy (himself a photographer) was highly indignant when Mr. W. H. Harrison suggested in the "Spiritualist" (June 5th, 1874) that "if Mr. Hudson sincerely regrets his past misdeeds, he should reveal the names of his accomplices to the National Association."†

"If," wrote Mr. Guppy,‡ "the National Association conceives itself empowered, and considers itself bound to inquire into all cases of imposition in Spiritualism, it had better advertise to that effect, and organize a court and jury, and appoint a judge, say Serjeant Cox; and if it do, will

---

* "The Spiritualist," January 15th, 1875.
† "Exposure" is a red rag to a bull with certain Spiritualists, especially if they be photographers!
‡ In the "Medium and Daybreak," June 12th, 1874.

Mr. Harrison appear before that court and confess 'his regret for any past misdeeds, and reveal the names of his accomplices'?

"Now, there is another thing. For a long time past the 'Spiritualist,' *i.e.*, Mr. W. H. Harrison, has been always 'harping' on sham photographs and Mr. Hudson. Some people said to me that it was done in a spirit of persecution. I replied, 'That may be true; but there are some grounds.' But really and truly, after that celebrated manifesto of Hudson's, no one had any right to say anything. Hudson published, 'I don't guarantee any spirit photographs,' and he made every person sign a book that they would ask no questions, or something to that effect. Well, after that, nobody had any right to comment. Hudson sold his spirit photographs as Tattersall sells his horses, 'with all faults.'

"Any one looking at the comments on Mr. Buguet's photographs, and that they bear the marks of being sham ones, and the comments on the New York spirit photographs, must see that it is absolutely necessary that some satisfactory method should be found to insure the reality of so important a phase in Spiritualism; and therefore, to print a venomous paragraph against Hudson, by name, at the moment of his misfortunes, and at the time when he has given a pledge never more to be concerned in a sham photograph, indicates a littleness of mind which is to be regretted in the case of the editor of a paper."

You see what a happy family Spiritualism is! and how easily even the known frauds of supposed friends of the cause are overlooked by some of the "faithful." The en_forced promise that the naughty boy will never do the like again wipes off all old scores, gives full absolution, and allows the "unfortunate" one to begin again *de novo*. Further than that even, the error is regarded in the light of a blessing, inasmuch as "the sham spirit photos, and the low price they were sold at, were the means of directing public attention to the subject to an extent which never would have occurred *if genuine photos only had been taken.*"*

In June, 1875, a remarkable trial took place before the Correctional Tribunal of Paris, which resulted in the conviction of certain "spirit photographers." The fraud was planned and carried out by one Buguet, who kept a photographic studio at No. 5 Boulevard Montmartre; Leymarie, Editor of the "*Revue Spirite,*" in which Buguet was be-puffed and his spirit photos published monthly; and an American medium, Firman, who assumed the *rôle* of spectre. Twenty francs was an ordinary fee for the production of spirit pictures—the portraits of deceased relatives or friends; but the knavish trio frequently received much larger sums. When customers came to the studio, they were (literally) taken in by a young lady cashier, who extracted their money and as many hints as possible as to the physiognomy of the spirit or person it was their desire to evoke. Then neighbours were called in to act the part of spirits; or plaster heads were decked out in the ghostly "properties" always kept in stock; or Firman presented his long-drawn visage as a ghost over the sitter's shoulder.

This nice little transaction ended in imprisonment, which is re-christened "persecution" by all right-feeling followers of the spirits.†

Mr. FEGAN EGERTON has long been known as a powerful medium, and "Jack Tod," the Liverpool spirit, "his

---

* "Medium and Daybreak," June 12th, 1874.
† See "Persecution of Spiritualists in Paris" in "The Spiritualist" for last half of 1875.

control," has enjoyed a world-wide reputation. Unhappy being, reader, if you knew not that before! But "there are more things in heaven and earth, Horatio, than are dreamt of in our philosophy!"

Well, I know not whether Mr. "Jack Tod" or his medium had offended the Liverpool Psychological Society, or Mr. John Lamont, its Vice-President; but certain it is they took the very unusual course (for them) of laying a trap for Egerton, and Virtue (represented by the "Vice") unmasked the "poor but (dis)honest" medium. The story is very well and truly told in the " Liverpool Daily Courier."* The *séance* was held at the " Spiritual Centre," in Russell Street.

" The circle was arranged, re-arranged, finally adjusted, and a due amount of hymn-singing was engaged in to get up the 'power.' Such hymns as ' The Banks of the Beautiful Spirit-Shore,' ' The Bright Summer Land,' ' Beautiful Star,' &c., were sweetly chanted, the sitters having, according to conditions, joined hands. All this time the medium was seated in the 'cabinet,' which was formed by screening off a niche in the apartment. This cabinet had been previously inspected with the utmost care, and was found to be quite satisfactory. As an extra precaution, prompted by some strange suspicion, Mr. Lamont had beforehand screwed the medium's chair fast down to the floor, so that there could be no possibility of his rising up and taking flight into Spiritland with the seat attached to his person. Added to all these precautions against deception was the tying of the medium in the chair by means of tape, which was done also by the cautious Mr. Lamont. In order, however, not to hamper the uses to which the obliging spirits might desire to put the medium, one arm was considerately left free, and this facility no doubt proved useful to Mr.

---

* November 26th, 1875.

Egerton in his subsequent performances. The gas was turned out; the 'conditions' were found to be favourable; 'Jack Tod' announced his presence, and gradually the work of materialization began. At first a dim speck of luminous vapour was visible; but by-and-bye the eager strained gaze of the sitters was able to descry a growing outline of something which became more and more defined, until—ah! there it was!—the indescribably beautiful spirit face of the previous *séance*, with the lovely gauze veil gracefully depending round the head and twined into a charming knot under the chin of the materialized spirit! There, too, was the marvellous 'phosphoric spirit light,' which glided and flickered about the face, now illuminating one lovely cheek and then another, as if the spirit had dexterously drawn its gas from its pocket, lighted the phosphoric taper, and was obliging the sitters with full and side views of its features! Several times, too, with reassuring consideration and intelligence, the head made a gentle bow, accompanied by an ineffably graceful smile, towards some one in the circle! These were the wonders believed to have been seen; the manifestation was complete, overwhelming—indubitable proof, first, of the medium's genuineness, and secondly, of the reality of materialization. Exclamations of delight escaped the entranced sitters, such as 'Glorious!' 'Marvellous!' 'Worth all your money!' (the price for admission to the *séance* was a shilling), when suddenly discord appeared in the circle. Mr. Lamont, who was nearest the medium, sprang from his place, and seizing Mr. Egerton round the body so as to pinion his arms, called for a light. There was a struggle; Mr. Lamont firmly kept his hold; and, after considerable confusion, the gas was relit. And lo! the disillusion! The medium was found holding in his hand an elegantly-constructed mask, representing a female face, upon the mask being arranged several yards of muslin of the texture of a butter-cloth. With these simple and innocent articles, aided by a few phosphoric matches, had the inspired medium constructed the marvellous spirit form of a few seconds before. Of course the *dénoûment* was utter confusion. The believers were hopelessly confounded; the medium, on being taxed with imposture, merely murmured, 'Well, well;' and finally, overwhelmed and astounded at their own foolishness, the audience dispersed in disgust. Before leaving, the 'medium' exonerated the proprietor of the establishment from all knowledge of or complicity in this trick; although he confessed that others, prominent local Spiritualists, were aware of it, and actually induced him to commit the imposture, and also that acts of simulation were invariably practised by professing mediums." So "Poor Jack" ("Tod") is in the doleful dumps for that "sweet little cherub" his medium, who now "sits up aloft" upon the stool of repentance.

The really serious point of the affair is the medium's statement that prominent Spiritualists had helped him to the imposture. Without giving too much credence to the word of such a man, our thoughts cannot but revert uneasily to a few revelations, and make us doubtful whether these practices may not be in vogue amongst some, at least, of those well-known and apparently respectable persons whose names appear so frequently at *séances*. The dread of exposing the medium in such persons is decidedly *suspicious;* but if we have a few more *contretemps* like the foregoing, "materialization" will soon go out of fashion, and deception and trickery—whether for love or money—need not be resorted to.

CHAPTER XI.

POOR "JOHN KING!"

A Materialization Theory—"John's" Earth-Life—A Bold Buccaneer—"A Pal of his"!—"The Boss"!—A "Jolly" Spirits' Song—"Baths and Bottled Stout"—Hair-brushing by Machinery—The Usual Failing !—Houndsditch Spirits—"A Professional Impostor"—"Coloured *Auras*"—A *Flighty* Medium—The Last of "John King"—Spirit Conjurors.

I AM in a position, by favour of the leading American Spiritual paper, the "Banner of Light," to state the method adopted for spirit "materialization":—"The human organism is constantly receiving accessions of new atoms in the process of rebuilding or recuperation, and is as constantly evolving in a vastly improved state those atoms which have been long enough in its organic association to become thus advanced or perfected . . . . The synthetic chemists of the other life 'electrify,' or otherwise control a great profusion of these evolving or sublimated atoms—enough to form, when condensed, a visible hand or arm . . . . In a moment, with the quickness of electricity, it may be, these atoms are again dismissed into 'thin air.'"

So much for *theory;* we shall find before this chapter is concluded that the *practice* is somewhat different.

Taken at the best these materialized spirit forms are a shady lot; they seldom stand more light than is indicated by "semi-darkness,"—which is very little light indeed!—and they have, usually, too much of the medium's face and voice to be quite beyond suspicion—save to the "faithful."

"'How can we prove the existence of these sperrits?' asked a sceptic of Mr. S. C. Hall. 'Prove them?' remarked S. C. impressively, 'the sperrits are above proof!'"*

From the "George Brown" of the Davenports to the "Minnie" of Miss Fairlamb there have been many spirit visitors in the flesh provided by their "synthetic chemists." There have been "black spirits and white, red spirits and grey," from "Zambia"—who declares that "although he has a black skin he has a white heart;" and who is able to be in two places at one time, "having appeared at the same hour to some Spiritualists in England, and to some others on board a ship on its way to New Zealand,"†—to "Florence Maple" (who gave a wrong address in Aberdeen), "Peter" the gardener, "Sweet William" the carpenter, and "John King," his wife, son, and daughter. The latter family, being the best-known of all the spirits, will demand special notice. I shall first give all that is known of "John" in "earth-life," and afterwards his rise and fall as a spirit. His name, it seems, upon the "rudimentary sphere," was "Sir Henry Morgan;" but whether he was the bold buccaneer who obtained letters of marque from Charles II., or whether he lived in Elizabeth's reign, is a point still unsettled. Pirate or not, he must have borne a bad character enough; he "does not like to revive memories of the past," and his statement that Sir Walter Raleigh was a "pal" of his, would seem to require further proof. He was possessed of "a forcible and uncontrollable disposition," and if the spirit picture be a portrait, was "swarthy in hue, almost like an Eastern,

---

* "Punch."
† "Spiritualist," May 15th, 1870.

with features of a not very large type, but handsome character; nose slightly aquiline, eyes dark, eyebrows and moustache well marked and defined, but not thick; and these, together with the thick bushy beard, of an intensely black colour, the lips thin, and mouth well formed; the head surmounted by a white, peculiarly shaped turban, the ends of which hung down on either side a broad, powerful chest, suggestive of the deep, sonorous tones of the voice of the owner."*

His wife and daughter, both called "Katey" in the spirit world, his son "John," his servant "Peter," who serves the "boss," as he calls "Sir Henry," with great devotion, and the old sea-dog himself, form a striking spirit group.

"Sir Henry" or "John" is, in the spirit as in the flesh, restless and energetic. Mr. Burns, who has the private lives of, and back-stair tittle-tattle about, all the spirits, says of him:

"'John King' has been identified with the work of Spiritualism from the earliest years of the movement. He produced physical manifestations in the family of Mr. Koons, in the backwoods of America, as related in Emma Hardinge's 'History of Spiritualism.' He also became identified with the work of the Davenport Brothers, and latterly manifested through the mediumship of Messrs. Herne and Williams, by which he is best known in this country."

Some Spiritualists consider "John" to be a kind of phantom, springing up like a Jack-in-the-box in the most out-of-the-way places; but Mr. Burns, who has "met him very frequently," says "he is as truly an individual as any of the persons about him," and he has me with him heartily in this!

---

* "Medium and Daybreak," August 8th, 1873.

"King" is a facetious spirit, and occasionally, in a "mischievous" humour, assuring Mr. Harrison that he "ought to look upon Spiritualism as a jolly thing. I'm jolly enough ! Look here, now ! I'll sing you a song of my own composition :

> I wish I had a bird,
> I would stick it on a spit, &c."

"John" also recommended a new inquirer to take regular baths, and a bottle of "Guinness's stout" every day at dinner. While his rubbing a paper tube over the inquirer's head, saying, "This is hair-brushing by machinery," and his remark, "Look here, Harrison, I have been put to do this work of convincing mortals for a certain number of years to work out my own salvation, and as I have to do it, I think it as well to make myself jolly over it," is as little *spiritual* as his advice. "He then," says Mr. Harrison, "began to whistle in a devil-may-care kind of way . . . . I put several mental questions to the spirits at this *séance.* They could not answer them, and were evidently unable to read my thoughts. . . . Mrs. Marshall also told me that spirits sometimes brought fruits to *séances* when fruits were asked for by the sitters. I remarked, 'Then I should like to ask for some tropical fruit not to be found on this side of the globe.' John King replied, 'So you may ;' upon which I said, 'Thank you ;' whereupon John King added, 'But you won't get it !'"*

The "John King" of the Marshalls (whose "sperrits is gone" for ever, now !) was, beyond all other "Johns," notorious for the untruthfulness of his statements. He declared himself to be a "native of Caermarthen," but did not display any local knowledge of that town. Sometimes —by accident, I presume—he managed to speak the truth,

---

* "Spirit People."

as when he allowed that spirit lights are mainly produced by phosphorus, and that the tilting of a table more on one side than another shows an excess of power upon that side! Notwithstanding "John's" hard work (he has done more than all the other materialized ones put together) and his indiscretion, he did for a long time escape detection, but now, alas! has gone the way of all spirits, *down*, and the story of his fall will be shortly told in these pages fresh as it comes from Liverpool—terror of materializing media!

Mr. FRANK HERNE (whose partnership with Mr. Chas. E. Williams is now a thing of the past) has been connected with more than one remarkable exposure anent "materialization." Considerable excitement was produced in London when Messrs. Herne and Williams first materialized hands, then faces, and afterwards the full form of "John King," who conversed with the sitters. The partners made money, and "all went merry as a marriage bell" until the latter end of 1872, or early in 1873, they were engaged to give their performance at Hull, when Herne—having the usual failing of the media, *spirits* — spoiled the "show." Williams waxed wroth at this, and declined any further connection with the recalcitrant one, who, in re-revenge, exposed the means whereby the "ghosts" were produced, and told how the spirit masks might be procured at a certain shop in Houndsditch! Of course this had no further effect upon the faithful than getting the spirituous being into disgrace; for nothing is more distasteful to your devout believer in Spiritualism than the awkward truth!

Mr. Burns lashed the naughty medium well, and declared that "according to his own confession he is a professional impostor, a cheat, and quite willing to make a living by receiving money under false pretences."*

---

* "Medium and Daybreak," April 4th, 1873.

Now, without quarrelling with our editorial friend over this matter (because "them's my sentiments!") I would point out the incongruous fact that almost immediately after this denunciation of the too Frank medium, we find Brothers Herne and Burns hob-nobbing at the "Spiritual Institution" (proprietor, Mr. B.), where "very powerful phenomena" are obtained; and to this day Mr. Herne is "manifesting" at the spirit *rendezvous* in Southampton Row, under the *ægis* of his former castigator!

Mr. Herne sees "coloured *auras*" around people; thus green does not denote the gullibility usually supposed to appertain to that colour, but is indicative of wickedness; blue, of course, shows wisdom, and red is love. He has been "levited," in open daylight too, this spirituous being! Not that any one can say—with Mr. Maccabe's countryman, "I seed it mysel'!"—but it is vouched for by the *flighty* medium that he was "caught away" whilst walking in "merrie Islington," and conveyed into the house of Mrs. Guppy, No. 1 Norland Villas, Highbury Hill Park, by invisible agency!* Could Mrs. G. do less than pay a return visit in the following year, to Lamb's Conduit Street (using the same mysterious locomotive power) after that it†

But poor Mr. Herne is in hot water again, and this time at Liverpool,‡ where Mr. John Fraser—the medium hunter —detected him with singular intrepidity and skill. And this is how Mr. Frank Herne and "poor John King" fell. Mr. Herne had been engaged to counteract the bad effects of the Egerton exposure, "to wipe out the stain caused by the false medium, rehabilitate the damaged

---

* May 20th, 1870.

† See Chapter IX.

‡ At that same spiritual centre, No. 38 Russell Street, where Mr. (Buttercloth) Egerton came to grief.

fabric of the belief, and silence once and for ever the blatant sceptics."

Six *séances* were arranged: at one of these the spirit of Harriet Lane* addressed the circle, beginning with the words, " Garlanded with the dowry of shame," whilst the faithful present whispered, " Ay, that's Harriet Lane: the Lord be praised!" Then the spirit of a Somersetshire man controlled the medium, and being asked in what sphere the murdered woman was, replied, " She be in a very foin spere, she be. Vurst she vuz not in such a good place, but hur'll be better by-and-bye, hur will. Hur was a black spirit when she coom vurst; hur be now a grey spirit; and hur'll soon be a white one." And then there was the " materialization" of a baby form, merely a newspaper rolled up and grasped by the medium to give the shape of the body, but which in the dim light one poor woman took to be the angel form of her loved and lost infant.

But the eventful evening came when "John King" was to be revealed in the full glare of the gas, and we may let the Liverpool " Daily Courier"† tell how his spiritship stood the light.

" Several gentlemen had formed a very strong opinion as to the utter imposture of the whole thing. There was but one chance remaining, and that not availing, the spiritualists would have achieved a great result. However, the fates were in other directions, and the spirits themselves must have played against the spirit-conjurors. The eager circle gathered together for a final manifestation. The stockbroker was there, hoping probably to get some augury that would help in his speculations; the master-carterish individual was also present, drinking in the wonders with

---
* Henry Wainwright's victim in the Whitechapel murder.
† Of Christmas Day, 1875.

great relish; there likewise was the dapper young gentleman who had come in his gymnasium dress, labouring, it is believed, under the delusion that the gigantic spirit was that of a noted ex-pugilist named King, with whom he was eager to have a 'set to.'" There was also a strange and "much spectacled" individual present. After the popular "Hold the Fort," "Shall we gather at the river," &c., were sung, and one or two manifestations produced, the *pièce de résistance* of the evening was forthcoming in the person (or spirit) of John King, "first as if tentatively selecting his position, and eventually appearing full at the aperture in the curtains. This was the critical moment: the strange man in spectacles bounded like a panther towards the cabinet, and made a grab at the spirit. The white drapery, or whatever it might be, was seen to shrivel up as if vanishing away. 'Gracious heavens! could it be a spirit after all?' was the question that overwhelmed for the moment the minds of the spectators. But at the same instant, the b..…y person already described as a master carter sprang from his seat and seized the medium on the left-hand side, so that the hapless impostor was thus caught in a vice. A howl of terror escaped his lips, and as the gas was being turned on another conspirator against the spirits made a dash at the cabinet, and brought the whole arrangement to the floor. The medium was handed out, and disclosed a most ludicrous make-up. About two yards of tarlatan was arranged round his head turbanwise, and covered him in front down to the thighs. On each leg was tied loose a newspaper—both copies of the 'Daily Courier' —and these served as the spirit's pantaloons; in the full blaze of the gaslight they reminded one of the top boots of a brigand in a melodrama. When dragged into the light, the terrified medium was still clutching one end of the strip of tarlatan, doubtless thinking his spirit dress would be some protection to him against the violence of the sceptics."

The medium, when asked to explain these slightly suspicious circumstances, replied that the scarf found upon him was undoubtedly his property, but how it or the newspapers came there he could not say; some person might have brought it in out of his bed-room, or it might have been conveyed in by the spirits. However, the sitters expressed in no mild terms that the whole thing was imposture of the grossest kind.

Yet what think you has Mr. Burns the effrontery to do? Why, "warmly urge the prosecution of the offenders!"—not the medium and his accomplices, mark you, but those who had exposed the fraud! Mr. B. even opened a subscription for this purpose; but so little money came in, it was changed into a testimonial of £15 (!) to Mr. Herne.

Time was that when a light was struck (the story ran), the medium would die; but *now*—we find sudden illuminations have no other effect than exposing frauds *which even Spiritualists themselves sometimes foster.*

When there is such an easy way of settling the truthfulness or falsity of the pretensions of materializing media as a light suddenly struck, why do the faithful neglect to take such ordinary precautions against imposition in what is, to them, so momentous a matter?

CHAPTER XII.

"SWEET KATEY KING!"

Little Florrie—"Dialectical" Whiskers—The Professor—"Lights down"—Enter "Katey King"—Photographing a Spirit—A "Scientist" *far gone*—"Sitting for Faces"—A little *faux pas*—Katey in America—Her "Earthli fe" History—The little Widow—Mrs. Holmes is "cick"—"Sweet Katey King"—The Philadelphia collapse.

MRS. ELGIE CORNER, *née* Miss Florence Cook, who for a time ruled amongst the faithful, was introduced to the "materialization" business early in life; and when the little lady was sweet sixteen, she had the honour of presenting "spirit faces" to the English people. There was "the Haverfordwest Spirit," and "Alphonse," whose surname—like William's in "Black Eyed Susan"—is unknown.

But the great hit which has given Miss Florrie a worldwide reputation was the materialization of Annie Morgan, or "Katey King"—that "delicate, ladylike, æsthetic individual, with fine features, abundance of auburn hair, and altogether interesting and *spirituelle* individuality."* This spirit frequently left the cabinet, and took her (or its) "walks abroad" among the assembled "sitters," conversing with them affably and shaking their hands. Instead of pur-

---

* Mr. Burns in "The Medium."

chasing a genuine spirit face in Houndsditch, like Messrs. Herne and Williams were wont to do, Miss Cook was content to present her own pretty Jewish one; but this never raised a doubt in the minds of the more "advanced" Spiritualists until a "dialectical gentleman, Mr. William Volckman, sceptically anxious to obtain a nearer view of the spirit physiognomy, which was indistinct in the 'dim religious light' of the *séance*-room, was rash and ungallant enough to spring from his chair and grasp her round the waist, thereby satisfying himself, as he says, that Katey and Miss Cook were indeed and in truth but one and the same person.

"It would be in vain to attempt to describe the *tableau* —terminating, not in the orthodox *red fire*, but by the sudden extinguishment of the gas—which followed. The unfortunate ghost must have had rather a critical time of it before it could be extricated from the grasp of Mr. Volckman by the combined efforts of a Justice of the Peace, a ship's officer, and a gentleman rejoicing in the appropriate name of 'Tapp,' who gallantly rushed to the rescue, and brought Mr. Volckman heavily to the ground, at considerable damage to that gentleman's neck, elbow, and knee. The ghost also, instead of 'dissolving in thin air,' tore hair from Mr. Volckman's beard, a hirsute ornamentation upon which the owner says he prided himself considerably."*

As it has been my endeavour all through this book to give the accounts of eye-witnesses of the phenomena— whether they be of the "elect" or the sceptical—I cannot do better than extract from the Rev. C. Maurice Davies's†

---

* J. H. in "Bell's Weekly Messenger."
† The reverend gentleman is on the Council of the British National Association of Spiritualists.

excellent work—"Mystic London" his report of these manifestations in Hackney:

"Two rooms communicated through folding-doors—the front apartment being that in which we assembled, and the back used as a bed-room, where the ladies took off their 'things.' This latter room, be it remembered, had a second room communicating with the passage, and so with the universe of space in general. One leaf of the folding-doors was closed, and a curtain hung over the other. Pillows were placed on the floor just inside the curtain, and the little medium, who was nattily arrayed in a blue dress, was laid upon them. We were requested to sing and talk during 'materialization,' and there was as much putting up and lowering of the light as in a modern sensation drama. The professor* acted all the time as master of the ceremonies, retaining his place at the aperture; and, I fear, from the very first, exciting suspicion by his marked attention not to the medium, but to the ghost. When it did come, it was arrayed according to orthodox ghost fashion, in loose white garments, and I must confess with no resemblance to Miss C.† We were at the same time shown the recumbent form of the pillowed medium, and there certainly was something blue, which might have been Miss C., or only her gown going to the wash.

"By-and-bye, however, with 'lights down,' a bottle of phosphorized oil was produced, and by this weird and uncanny radiance, one or two privileged individuals were led by the 'ghost' into the back bed-room, and allowed to put their hands upon the entranced form of the medium. I was not of the 'elect,' but I talked to those who were, and

---

* Mr. William Crookes, F.R.S.
† But "Katey" was not always unlike the medium; indeed, the spirit has been known to apologize for the awkward resemblance between the two faces.

their opinion was that the 'ghost' was a much stouter bigger woman than the medium; and I confess that certain unhallowed ideas of the bed room door and the adjacent kitchen stairs connected themselves in my mind with recollections of a brawny servant-girl, who used to sit sentry over the cupboard in the breakfast-room—where was she?

"As a final *bonne bouche* the spirit made its exit from the side of the folding-door covered by the curtain, and immediately Miss C. rose up with dishevelled locks in a way that must have been satisfactory to anybody who knew nothing of the back door and the brawny servant, or who had never seen the late Mr. Charles Kean act in the 'Corsican Brothers' or the 'Courier of Lyons.'

"I am free to confess the final death-blow to my belief that there might be 'something' in the face manifestations, was given by the effusive professor, who has 'gone in' for the double with a pertinacity altogether opposed to the calm judicial examination of his brother learned in the law,* and with prejudice scarcely becoming a F.R.S."

The F.R.S., whose peculiar enthusiasm is little in keeping with careful investigation, was rewarded for his faith by Katey's unreserved confidence, which, he says, "gradually grew until she refused to give a *séance* unless I took charge of the arrangements. She said she always wanted me to keep close to her and near the cabinet, and I found that after this confidence was established, and she was satisfied I would not break any promise I might make to her, the phenomena increased greatly in power, and tests were freely given that would have been unobtainable had I approached the subject in another manner. She often consulted me about persons present at the *séances*, and where they should be placed, for of late she had become

---

* Serjeant Cox.

very nervous, *in consequence of certain ill-advised suggestions that force should be employed as an adjunct to more scientific modes of research."**

The F.R.S. succeeded by the aid of the electric light in photographing "Katey King," the innocent spirit—true daughter of Eve—being very curious about "that queer machine," the camera; and the scientific gentleman indulged in the following "gush" upon her loveliness:

" But photography is as inadequate to depict the perfect beauty of Katey's face, as words are powerless to describe her charms of manner. Photography may, indeed, give a map of her countenance; but how can it reproduce the brilliant purity of her complexion, or the ever-varying expression of her most mobile features, now overshadowed with sadness when relating some of the bitter experiences of her past life, now smiling with all the innocence of happy girlhood when she had collected my children round her, and was amusing them by recounting anecdotes of her adventures in India?

> 'Round her she made an atmosphere of life,
>   The very air seemed lighter from her eyes,
> They were so soft and beautiful, and rife
>   With all we can imagine of the skies;
>   Her overpowering presence made you feel
>   It would not be idolatry to kneel.'"†

The "scientist" who writes like this—and clasps the beautiful and substantial spirit in his arms—is much too far gone for "investigation"!

But the hour of parting was to come, and Katey was to materialize no longer, Miss Cook retiring from that portion of the business. Katey, unfortunately, appeared afterwards

---

* "The Spiritualist," June 5th, 1874. (A brave man, indeed, would be required for any unscientific research, *if he wore whiskers!*)
† "The Spiritualist," June 5th, 1874.

in America, and there—like the pitcher that goes too often to the well—"came to grief!"

Mr. and Mrs. HOLMES had "sittings for faces," at No. 16 Old Quebec Street, Oxford Street, and were wondrously successful in 1873; the three *séances* weekly which these distinguished professors of the Spiritual Art gave being overcrowded. Fortune was smiling, and the golden harvest was being garnered in, when suddenly, by a turn of the fickle goddess's wheel, the idols were thrown down, and became (in England at least) discredited media. The little *faux pas* was brought about by a light struck unexpectedly, which revealed Mrs. Holmes out of her place, and "Nelson" (Mr. H.)—who, like he of Trafalgar, had only one hand available, the other being held by some person in the circle—wildly gyrating a guitar above his head, and so producing the ghostly music. This exposure, for which all materializing media must be prepared, led to us losing "Nelson" and his clever wife, for they left London shortly after and retired to America. You might think they would now retire from the "profession" also; but, no! An exposure or two cannot weaken the faith of the few; so in the land of the Stars and Stripes the loving couple were soon hard at work drawing the "higher intelligences" from their spheres and the dollars from Yankee pockets. No one thought of that slight peccadillo in the modern Babylon; none accused them of having knowingly deceived the "Britishers;" so they were on the top of the wheel once more.

"Katey King" having quitted London for "a higher sphere," true to her word, re-appeared in a second floor, Ninth Street, Philadelphia. In this exalted region she was the "familiar" of the Holmeses; who, though banished from England to "repint of their sins," were here doing a fine trade in spirit production. "Katey" created a great sensation; though neither good-looking or accomplished, she was run after for her beauty and lauded for her ability.*

All the newspapers in America contained lengthy accounts of the Holmes's *séances*, and glowing descriptions of their beautiful visitant, who was declared to have the same features as the Katey King seen in England. Mr. Leslie's account† runs thus:

"Although set down as a denizen of the other world, Katey seemed to us to be as objective a reality as ever trod this earth. She walked among us, permitted us to touch her hands and her white robe; spoke to us in good round modern English, which we considered somewhat extraordinary, seeing that she lived upwards of two hundred years ago, when the quaintness of Spenser overshadowed her native tongue. . . . She wore a white robe of some singular fabric, and a light drab veil wound gracefully about her head. The folds of her dress concealed her feet, but her arms were bare, and, like her figure, exquisitely moulded. Her complexion was absolutely transparent, and her hair, instead of being dark as generally represented, was, in our opinion, auburn with a golden tinge. She wore no ornaments, and after remaining with us four or five minutes, and making a few very commonplace observations, she re-entered the cabinet without closing the door. Here she stood facing us for a few seconds, when Mrs. Holmes asked her whether she could disappear before the visitors as she had done on

---

* She gave full particulars of her birth, parentage, &c., to Dr. Child. She was born in London, May 12th, 1660. (Miss Cook's Katey said she was born and lived in Wales!) Her father was passionate, irritable, and intemperate in his habits (Oh, John!), and the young lady herself had not acted with that rigid propriety expected of an English lady. See "The Spiritualist," August 28th, 1874.

† "Leslie's Illustrated Newspaper."

former occasions. To this interrogatory she made the same reply as she had to the other; and, surprising to relate, gradually faded away into thin air before us, until not a vestige of her was to be seen."

The newspaper people were not the only sane persons taken in by what turned out to be an imposition, the Hon. Robert Dale Owen, who had followed the beloved spirit of Katey from England, being amongst the gulled ones.

But the scene was to change. Through the intimacy of the Holmeses with a widow who desired to be known, if at all, as "Mrs. White," they had been enabled to present to "the 'cutest nation on airth" their celebrated ghost, "Katey King," and to run that sensation for a considerable time; but being behindhand in their payments, the business-like spirit had declined to "materialize" any longer, until the following letter brought "Dear Frank" or "Mrs. White" back again.

"DEAR FRANK,—I wish I could see you to-day. It is very dull here in this little town (Blissfield). Nelson is ritten too and I expect he will rite all the news to you you need not be afraid of our not dooing the fair thing with you for we shall. I have been quite cick and am not able to set up now but thought I must rite a few lines to you. I got dispointed in gitting the money that I told you I expected. I found my brother in poor circumstances so he could not pay me eney thing but Nelson" (Mr. Nelson Holmes) "says he will send you fifty dollars next week then you had better cum as soon as you get this. How is Sam getin along let me know. A kiss for you, from

"JENNIE HOLMES.

"exkuse this for I am cick to-day love to Sam I must tell you something good Nelson and I have been very good to each other we have not had a cross werd since we left home that makes me feel glad and you will sympathise with me won't you dear Frank."

"Mrs. White" went to Blissfield and "materialized" as usual, but the spirit came in such a "questionable shape" that suspicions were raised. Several of the inhabitants, believing the "materialization" to be a fraud, watched the house in which the Holmeses lodged, and when a stranger, dressed as a man, hove in sight, their suspicions were aroused by a remarkable likeness between this person and the spirit of "sweet Katey King." They managed to capture the "man" after a free fight, in which "he" broke a cane over the heads of the assailants: this "man" turned out to be Mrs. White, the veritable "Katey King."

It was reserved for Philadelphia, however, to complete the exposure of the manner in which the Holmeses obtained money by false pretences.*

"The full account of the discovery of the shallow trick of the Holmeses was contributed to our columns," says the "Philadelphia Inquirer," "by the gentleman who made it, and and from whom our representative obtained it through the agency of Dr. Child. It emanates, therefore, from the highest and best authority. . . . The gentleman above referred to failed to see how spirits could cover themselves with flesh and blood; in fact, to him such a thing 'stands not within the prospect of belief,' but he was still willing to be convinced if facts sufficient existed. One evening when in proximity to 'Katey,' he ascertained she had a bad breath, which produced rather an unfavourable impression; but still he reflected that a lady who had been dead

---

* Alas! *they* had no devoted *savant*, no F.R.S., to stand sentry by the cabinet door, or defeat the "prying" investigation which brought about the following terrible collapse.

two hundred years ought to have a bad breath, and he was unwilling

> 'To bear the tidings of calamity,
> Like an unseasonable stormy day,'

to others, and for the time remained quiet; in other words, 'submitted to the conditions' imposed upon all the frequenters of the Spiritual sanctum. Believing that 'flesh and blood cannot enter the kingdom of heaven,' and too gallant to believe that Miss King was spiritually in "'tother place,' the aforesaid gentleman concluded that Katey must be 'to the manner born.' The admirers of Katey were neither few nor far between. In fact, the young lady had been loaded with presents; rings, lockets, pearl crosses, beads, love-letters, &c., had been freely bestowed. No modern belle or acknowledged beauty could have received more attention than did Katey. A number of those who came under her influence, got to writing poetry in her honour, some of it by what Spiritualists call 'impression.' Some of this poetry was just as wretched as could possibly be put together by presumably sane people. The following is a sample:

> 'Oh, gather 'round and let us sing
> The praises of sweet Katey King,
> Who from her bright and happy sphere
> Comes smiling to us mortals here.
> CHORUS.—Then with glad voices let all sing
> The praises of sweet Katey King.'

"Although the evidences of the 'machine made' verse are in the above, many of the other inspired lines are much worse as to tune, sentiment, metre, and rhythm . . .

"Things were going on smoothly; money was flowing into the coffers of the 'mediums,' and Katey's friends were jubilant at the number of converts daily being made to the cause of 'spirit materialization;' but suddenly, without warning, Katey disappeared. Night after night her devotees assembled to welcome her return. The 'medium' with plaintive voice sang 'I am coming; I am coming;' but she did *not* come. Various were the reasons assigned. Some said 'she was offended at unkind remarks that had been made about her.' The 'mediums' said that 'some rude fellows had entered the cabinet and taken all the magnetism out;' and, furthermore, that Katey had ascended to a 'higher sphere' and exhausted her strength; others were uncharitable enough to say that 'Katey was on strike.'

"In the meantime, the gentleman who was seeking knowledge under difficulties had been making extraordinary exertions to find her daily whereabouts—otherwise, her boarding-house. Little by little he quietly picked up information that enabled him to find a young lady whom he thought very much resembled Katey King. Using the most detective-like skill, he followed his clue up successfully. By certain peculiarities which he observed in the Katey of the other world at the *séances*, he found that a young woman who resembled Katey generally, and had her peculiarities, took her meals with great regularity at a certain house which he had 'piped off,' in detective parlance. He then shadowed this woman, and found that she attended all the *séances* at the Holmes's house. He ultimately concluded to scrape an acquaintance with Katey in the flesh, choosing as an auspicious time an hour when the lady of materializing tendencies had been rendered happy by a good, square, worldly meal. The first interview was a failure; the supposed Katey protested that she 'did not believe in Spiritualism'—declared that she had seen the manifestations at Holmes's but once, and, so 'far as she knew, they were all right.' These assertions, however, did not satisfy the earnest seeker after truth, and various schemes, devices, plans, and promises were resorted to in the hope of discovering some of the many 'presents' that had been made to Katey. Through patience, perseverance, and certain considerations, one present was produced. This satisfied the gentleman that he was in the right place. More patience, perseverance, and promises, and out dropped another, and so on until a small table was covered with rings, lockets, crosses, beads, and robes worn in the different 'spheres' from which Katey had kindly descended to visit mortals at so much *per capita*. The object of the gentleman's efforts was to so narrow down the evidences of fraud that he might be able to 'knock the bottom' out of the humbug at a blow, and here was his object attained. Here was not only the veritable Katey weepingly acknowledging her duplicity, but producing 'material' evidences of it in the shape of all those little tokens of regard which she had been fondly believed to have borne off in her spirit shape to her abode in the other 'spear,' as most of the 'affected' term it . . . The gentleman improvised a *séance*. Procuring a suitable apartment, to which he invited a number of 'Katey's' friends, he arranged with the lady, who now acquiesced in his suggestion for her appearance, dressed in the gauzy fabric and other trappings she used to disport herself in at Holmes's shows. She did so, a sort of cabinet being hastily improvised, and the exposure was rendered complete, beyond a chance of cavil or dispute. As a result there are a few Spiritualists who are better and wiser men and women, and, as a still better result, a check was administered to a most dangerous excitement which was beginning to affect the minds of thousands of superficial thinkers, as it had already weakened those of many men and women who believed all too willingly in the trickery of designing, greedy New Yorkers of the true 'Yankee' stripe."

This was a death-blow to the Holmeses in America, and

even their firmest adherents drew back. Dr. Child, writing to Miss Emily Kislingbury* (February 15th, 1875), says, "I thank you for your expression of sympathy in regard to the abominable fraud which the Holmeses have practised upon us. They would not have succeeded so well if we had not had great confidence in the interesting reports we have had from London of your Katey, which they very shrewdly imitated in almost every particular, and were thus better able to carry on their wicked deception. It is all over now, and what does it amount to? Simply that two base tricksters—clever, it is true—have succeeded in deceiving many of us for several months. Now they admit a part of their fraud."

---

* The lady who guides the destinies of the *Foreign Office*,—at the British National Association of Spiritualists.

CHAPTER XIII.

ODDS AND ENDS.

The Fourth Estate—Ghostly *forms*—Stone-throwing Spirits—"No Spiritual Organ pays"—Tweedledum and Tweedledee!—The Progress of Fanaticism—The Spiritual Army—Horace Greeley on the Constitution—The Lost Bird—Wonderful Shadows!—A poor Judge!—A Villa in the Spheres—The "Screechy Chair"—Poor Owen!—"Iota"—Scientific Investigation—Serjeant Cox on Materialization—A Prop to the "Pantheon"—Early Crookean views—*Blind Faith* v. *Precaution*—An F.R.S.'s Investigations—The "Dialecticals"—"To Proprietors of Haunted Houses."

THE FOURTH ESTATE.

THE Spiritual "organs" are ever busily engaged in grinding the same deadly-lively tune, and their supernatural "gush" is very wearisome. From America some *spirited* and racy items come occasionally to brighten up these ghostly "forms," and even a flutter of excitement may quicken the "circulation" of the stagnant periodicals, when a little home news, such as "Stone-throwing Spirits,"* is reported from Hampton Wick (the wick-ed ghosts thus having revenge for the removal of their bones!); but this soon subsides when the real hero of the window-smashing

---

* "The Spiritualist," September 18th, 1875.

exploits is proved to be, not a ghost, but a little boy, who receives one month's imprisonment with hard labour,* as a reward for his zealous work in the interests of the glaziers.

We can account, now, for the terribly low state of the Spiritualistic press, for Mr. Burns has let that unexpected cat—the truth—out of his editorial bag, thus : "*No spiritual organ pays.*"† The " Medium " is in low—and its editor frequently in hot—water, and we hear from him "that all the other (Spiritual) publications are carried on at a loss, with, perhaps, the exception of ' Human Nature,' *the most successful and high-toned of our serials,*‡ and which about meets expenses.

Here is a fearful state of things ! and all this, notwithstanding the wonderful strides Spiritualism is taking ! Do the seven-leagued boots of Spiritualism walk *backwards*, though ? When the new religion first began to "feel the ground" in England, the " Spiritual Magazine " was started (January, 1860), and since that time many periodicals have sprung up, all to meet with the bitter experience that "the flourishing condition of Spiritualism" meant—ruin ; and now, as a business speculation, not one can pay its way, but is dependent upon the charity, not exactly of the faithful few, but of the faithful and moneyed fewer ! All this, too, when the " Spiritualist " receives " enormous political subsidies," and the " Medium " swallows up the funds of the Spiritual Institution.

Is it not a wonder that the English people can be so blind to the merits of these papers? it is not so abroad, in the case of the " Medium," at any rate, for a Continental

---

* The "Daily Telegraph," September 28th, 1875.
†" Medium and Daybreak," July 9th, 1875.
‡ Modest man! you publish it.

correspondent says, "I read the 'Medium' with *great*, the 'Times' with *some* interest."*

Now, which of the weakly Spiritual newspapers must I name first? I am sure to offend one of the editors by giving precedence to the rival sheet, for there is a fierce and uncompromising warfare between "Tweedledum and Tweedledee."

Yielding to the claim of seniority *only* (so don't abuse me, Mr. Harrison), I begin with the "Medium and Daybreak." This paper was established as "Daybreak," in June, 1868, and in April, 1870, assumed its present title. Its pages are devoted to Spiritualism, the lunacy laws, and anti-vaccination.

Mr. Burns leads a busy life, for besides his editorial duties he conducts the Spiritual Institution, of which he is managing director, chairman, treasurer, secretary, and committee, and he has recently given the "People's Advocate" a terrible "wigging" for daring to mention this little fact; he says: "The 'People's Advocate' has a very foggy notion of what constitutes an institution. The Spiritual Institution is not one because it has neither committee nor officers, and Mr. Burns is its sole proprietor. It has 'officers,' very active ones, who are engaged continually in promoting Spiritualism and supplying inquirers with information. It has a committee of spirits; hence it is a 'Spiritual' Institution, and this 'committee' have made their work a world-wide success."

What a pity it is that Mr. Burns will not receive a testimonial; but no, *he will not have one!* And see how modestly he declines what nobody seems to have offered.

---

* The "Medium," June 11th, 1875.

"No Testimonial to J. Burns.

By my actions in the past I have lent my approval to testimonials, and they are good and appropriate to certain people, but not to me. What would we think of reading that Jesus the Christ had in His day become so respectable that He was presented with a bag of yellow dust and a flattering address from the men of Jerusalem and round about? That is not the reward for which spiritual men work, and it can never satisfy them as the fruits of their labour."*

Though averse to a testimonial, he is constantly appealing for assistance, now giving three columns of reasons why Spiritualists should "support Burns's business,"† or "give the shop a turn," or "do something for the good of the house." Then sometimes he becomes pathetic, and declares "Ours is a continued warfare, which must be prosecuted till victory is gained or all is lost. We are kept so deficient in means that it tells on our health sadly, and we are really offering ourselves up a living sacrifice that the work may go on. If our readers would make up their minds right away to raise us a fund of, say £1,000, we could go on and double our work, and have no further anxiety."‡

Noble man! Here he is ready to receive £1,000, and in the attitude of supplication we must leave him.

The "Spiritualist" newspaper — notwithstanding its crotchets, women's rights, &c.—is the most readable, respectable, and, generally, the best paper published in this

---

* "Medium and Daybreak," November 19th, 1875.
† "Mr. Burns and his business," says Dr. Clark, himself a Spiritualist, "is one of the evils of Spiritualism in London."
‡ "Medium," September 10th, 1875.

country in the interests of Spiritualism. It was started in the year 1869, and does not seem to have enjoyed a very prosperous career, being undersold by the "Medium and Daybreak." The editor of the "Spiritualist," Mr. W. H. Harrison, naturally complains when, "for the last six years, the public funds of Spiritualists, to the extent of thousands upon thousands of pounds, have been used without the knowledge of the donors in most desperate attempts to extinguish 'The Spiritualist' by underselling . . . . The money which has done us so much injury was for the most part subscribed by our personal friends and by the warm supporters of this journal, in response to incessant demands, the donors not knowing the effect of the method of expenditure."* And Mr. Burns returns this home-thrust by observing that "every person has been maligned at one time or another. I have had pretty considerable experience these last six years from one particular quarter, which will be recognized. I speak feelingly."† So, there is heart-burning in the midst of the Spiritualistic camp!

I hear that Mr. W. H. Harrison is to receive a testimonial for his "voluntary self-sacrifice of worldly interests." Mr. Burns says he "rejoices at the movement, because it tends to strengthen the claim which *we* have made upon the friends of the movement that they will aid us in our expenses. We hope this help will be carried out to the letter, *though Mr. Harrison has laboured hard to prevent our getting the absolute necessaries for our work.*"‡ Mr. Harrison has at least shown zeal *for the cause*, and, as far as I can judge, has been most unselfish in his devotion to it—sacrificing good worldly prospects for that miserable mess of pottage the editorship of a Spiritual newspaper.

---

* "The Spiritualist," July 23rd, 1875.
† "Medium," August 20th, 1875.
‡ "Medium and Daybreak," September 10th, 1875.

Mr. Harrison has recently published a work entitled "Spirit People," which his dear brother editor, Mr. Burns, describes as "a few columns of newspaper type-matter, printed on paper much too large—reminding the reader of a little boy in his father's garments."* It is a reprint of a paper read before an obscure association of inquirers into Spiritualism, but full of curious and—not to be irreverent—amusing matter. If any one has a morbid desire to see what very weak pegs a man may hang a faith upon, let him read this terribly candid editor's book. Mr. Harrison is not my enemy, therefore I do not rejoice that he has published what should be called "The Confessions of an English Spiritualist." His business way of recording the "phenomena" is out of all concord with the facility with which he is ever ready to accept the most trifling effects—mere conjuring tricks—as of supramundane origin. It is a pitiable plight for an able man to be thus bound, Mazeppa-like, to that "galled jade"—the spavined and bleareyed Rozinante of Spiritualism

A FAITHFUL FEW

are to be found clinging to the most preposterous beliefs; the Peculiar People, and Mrs. Girling's devoted band in the New Forest, being two modern instances of this fanaticism; and any one who cares to investigate the history of religious delusions will find plenty as full of absurdity as the Spiritualism of to-day.

The love of the marvellous may lead to a mental hallucination, which will annihilate common sense, and without wishing to be offensive to the amiable, conscientious, and —apart from Spiritualism—clever men and women in the

---

* "Medium and Daybreak," November 5th, 1875.

movement, I would suggest this fact as an explanation of their vagaries.

There is nothing new in such hallucination. Dr. Stone, in his work on the "Progress of Fanaticism," states that about the beginning of the present century, during an extensive religious excitement in Kentucky, many persons insisted upon the words of our Saviour being literally understood—"Except ye be converted and become as little children, ye cannot enter into the kingdom of heaven." Some commenced playing marbles in the church; an old lady took a side-saddle seat upon her umbrella, and cantered up and down the aisle; and an old gentleman, crossing a "fiery, untamed steed,"—his stick—rushed like a high-mettled racer to and fro, exclaiming joyfully, "Oh, my dear brethren and sistern, the childlike spirit carrieth me to heaven on a wooden hoss! Hallelujah!"

I think it was Archbishop Whately—said to be a Spiritualist himself—who wrote, "When people have resolved to shut their eyes, or to look only on one side, it is of little consequence how good their eyes may be." Certainly there is no bigotry so blinding as that of Spiritualism. That some clever men should have fallen into this error is indeed to be lamented; but the illustrious roll-call is not of great length, and the rank and file of the small Spiritualist army seems to be an ill-trained and ignorant rabble, presenting the very seamiest side of intellect.

It *is* rather hard that Spiritualists are usually taken to be either knaves or fools;* but so it is, and these peculiar folk have deliberately chosen their position, and set themselves against the good, sound common sense of the world.

---

* "There is something unpleasant in the alternative of knave or fool, when invited (as Spiritualists usually are) to select a character for themselves out of the pair."—Professor de Morgan.

Odds and Ends.

We have heard that

> "'T is pleasing at times to be slightly insane,"

and Horace Greeley has observed that "if a man will be a consumate jackass and fool, he is not aware of anything in the Constitution to prevent it," so the world can only look on in wonder, and mayhap pity, at such a spectacle. Some of the leaders of whom I shall have to speak may doubtless have seen the spectral illusions of which they write, and which may "arise from a highly excited state of the nervous irritability acting generally upon the system."* Of these, Judge Edmonds may be taken as a good specimen. Others have, in the simplicity of their hearts, been the gulls of designing media; and others again have succeeded in humbugging themselves.

It is no uncommon thing for disgraced and discredited media to be received again into the fold, and taken to the bosoms of the faithful once more, with reasoning such as this:

> "Sir, did that youth confess he had cheated me,
> I'd not believe him. He may cheat at times—
> That's in the 'medium' nature; thus they're made:
> Vain and vindictive, cowards, prone to scratch,
> And so all cats are; still, a cat's a beast;
> You coax the strange electric sparks from out
> By rubbing back its fur; not so a dog,
> Nor lion, nor lamb: 't is the cat's nature, sir!
> Why not the dog's? Ask God, who made them beasts!
> D'ye think the sound, the nicely-balanced man,
> Like me *(aside)* like you yourself *(aloud)*;
> He's stuff to make a medium? Bless your soul!
> 'T is these hysteric, hybrid half-and-halfs,
> Equivocal, worthless vermin, yield the fire!
> We must take them as we find them, 'ware their tricks,
> Wanting their service. Sir, Sludge took in you,
> How, I can't say, not being there to watch.

---

* "Sketches of the Philosophy of Apparitions." By S. Hibbert, M.D.

> He was tried, was tempted by your easiness.
> He did not take in me!" *

It is wonderful to note the credulity of even intelligent people; frequently at the Egyptian Hall the "materialized spirit" is addressed in an imploring tone by some of the faithful amongst the audience, with "John, John! speak to your old friend, John!" One lady has assured me that she can *see* spirits in the glass beneath *Psycho*, helping him in his arithmetic, his whist-playing, and his conjuring; and I have many strange visitors upon stranger errands. Not long ago a mysterious veiled figure, which I afterwards discovered to be that of an elderly lady, came to consult me as to how she should recover her lost bird. It seems poor "Dickey's" cage had been left open, and the bird had flown or been disposed of by the lodging-house cat—guilty perhaps in this instance, if not of all the petty larceny ascribed to that much-maligned animal. I told the old lady the simple fact, that I was not a clairvoyant, and quite unable to say what had become of her treasure. She was loth to believe this, and left, declaring that had she been in Paris she could easily have found a "wise woman," who could have told her all about it! When there are such simple people in the world, can we wonder that the demand should create a supply of spirit mediums, mesmerists, clairvoyants, crystal ball people, &c.?

Now, the "faithful" amongst the Spiritualists have got to such a pitch that the media are not subjected to tests at private *séances*, "which partake more of the character of a religious ceremony." Here, where the most wonderful phenomena are said to be produced, to name the hateful word "test" would be as great an indignity as asking your guests to turn their pockets inside out to show they were

---

* *Sludge the Medium.*

not kleptomaniacally inclined, or had not abstractedly abstracted the silver spoons.

And the wonderful things these faithful see; how easy they are of solution sometimes! Mr. Harrison tells of a lamp he constructed, and when it was placed upon the floor alight, great shadows were seen upon the opposite wall: weird and unearthly enough they looked; but when the cat was discovered rubbing herself against the warm glass, how the wonder vanished!

Indeed, the faithful are but as clay in the hands of the potter, and the mediumistic crew can mould them into any form they will. No wonder if the spirits call them "fools and asses"* for their pains.

The Hon. J. W. G. EDMONDS, late Judge in the Supreme Court of Appeal for the State of New York, has left a legacy of experiences in the spheres which would go far to impress the ordinary reader with his insanity, unless he more mercifully accepted the solution offered by the "Edinburgh Review" (October, 1865), which says, "His periodical visions of celestial nature, and the supposed communications made by spirits, are simply the results of self-induced somnambulism or hypnotic sleep. Such mental phenomena are perfectly reconcilable with well-known and established physiological and psychological principles."

The Judge is quite at home in those beautiful steps in the ladder to heaven, the spheres, which are Paradise itself. The spirit emancipated from the body has here all the enjoyments of this world without its care and sorrows, and each wears a crown of "solidified light"—the predominant colour being *green*, of course! Here all the sciences, and dancing, singing, sketching from nature, and

---

* "Spirit People."

whist-playing, are, according to Dr. Hare,* the usual occupations and amusements. What a haven for "Psycho!" How they would rattle his bones—that is, his machinery—with their eternal whist-playing!

Surely the Judge's experience of "the Summer Land" cannot easily be paralleled. He had seen spirits ranging in height from three inches to twenty feet; some had been eighteen thousand years in celestial spheres who yet retained the form of monkeys, while others had hoofs and horns, such as he had seen in pictures.

His wife's abode in the spirit world he found situated on the margin of a beautiful lake, whereon steamers were constantly plying. "It seems," said he, "that she had taken great pains to recall many of the scenes and things of earth which were associated with me and with pleasing remembrances; even her old rocking-chair, in which she had nursed all our children, and whose screeching they yet remember so well, and her work-table, which was one of the first articles of furniture I ever got her. . . . . While I was looking at these things a carriage and four horses drove up to the door. It was a beautiful turn-out. The carriage was light and tasty, with a high seat for the driver, and one seat behind for two persons. It was painted yellow, and on its panels was my seal! The harness was light and airy, and the horses were superb animals of the true Arabian breed, with long sleek bodies, clean limbs, and a springing motion to every step. They were well groomed, high-spirited, and well broke, and of different colours, being matched rather for quality than for looks. The presiding spirit and my wife entered the carriage, while I ascended the driver's seat, and took the reins from the coachman."†

---

* "Supernal Theology."
† "Spiritualism." By Judge Edmonds. Vol. II., page 134.

The Judge should really tell us whether the "presiding" one is a gentleman spirit or not, as the narrative is otherwise incomplete. Are there "spiritual marriages" in the "spheres"? (they have been in vogue on the "rudimentary," we know!)—and had the lady so far forgotten her earthly lord as to take an ethereal one to her arms? We should know the lady's character in earth-life, to tell whether our day-dreamer was a good judge in leaving matters as they were, without bother, even so; or perhaps being divorced from the flesh rids the spirit of all attendant obligations, and allows it to enter into fresh contracts!

If we have no certainty in all this, at least we find where the old furniture goes to! Or is it only the ghost of the "screeching" chair which the Judge's lady rocks herself upon? Can there be a spiritual Rag Fair, or a ghostly Moses and Son's, where aërial beings, intent upon visiting our earth, may go and get a "rig-out" to do so with decency? Alas! the Judge, while telling so much, neglects this important information.

The word of this "Sir Oracle" of Spiritualism might be taken with less suspicion, if we could forget the exposure of his adherence to that story, written in A. E. Poe's thrilling style, entitled, "The Eventful Nights of August 20th and 21st." Mr. James Gordon Bennett, in the "New York Herald," says, "The writer, Mr. F. C. Ewer, of San Francisco, took it into his head to prepare for the 'California Pioneer Magazine' a fiction of rather a bold and original conception, undertaking to describe the sensations of a dying man during the moment of dissolution, and sketching the scene which opens to the soul as it enters upon its second existence. Some two or three months after it was published, the writer was surprised by receiving a letter from Judge Edmonds, stating that he had copied the first part of it into the November number of the 'Sacred Circle,' and adding the astounding fact that he (the Judge) had had several spiritual interviews with the defunct fictitious hero of the narrative, 'John F. Lane'! The best part of the joke is, that the article contains assertions in physics which are impossible, and which, to minds less credulous than those of Judge Edmonds and his fellow-dupes, would have at once suggested doubts as to the sincerity of the writer. The value attached to the Judge's adhesion to the new sect will, after this exposure, be considerably lessened. If his present convictions have been arrived at on such loose evidence as the above, we can only say that, however much we may admire the extent of his faith, we can have very little respect for his professional acumen."

I don't know what the Spiritualists say to all this; perhaps they will insist that the story *should* have been true, as the "Spiritualist" (August 20th, 1875) wishes to claim "The Clergyman's Confession," by Wilkie Collins, as a genuine ghost story, "which has been introduced without comment, and which reads like many another spirit manifestation, agreeing with and corroborating the reality of what most Spiritualists have witnessed within the last two or three years. . . . . This clergyman's story shows that the writer is well acquainted with the phenomena of materialization, and we repeat that the story would have been more in place in the columns of our journal."

The Judge, shortly after his conversion to Spiritualism, became a medium, and through him Swedenborg wrote his name, spelling it "Sweedenborg," and adding, "who wrote so many foolish things on earth, which he is willing to rectify in the spirit." I wonder if "Edmonds is willing" to do the same! for the poor man passed into "spirit-life" on an Easter morning, happily relieved from the pains of the body and—as I think—the afflictions of his mind.

The HON. ROBERT DALE OWEN — perhaps as pure-minded a man as ever lived—has been a recent victim to the monstrous delusion of Spiritualism. As the "New York Tribune" says, "he was a man of singular purity and sincerity of character. His intellectual integrity was as unquestionable as his literary skill, and his conversation was as fascinating as his writing. Few of his friends attached much importance to his judgment, and most of them gently laughed at the strange notions to which he devoted so much time during his later years."

These "strange notions" he had set before the world in a work entitled "The Debatable Land," and this, with his "carefully arranged book of authentic facts," as Home calls the "Footfalls on the Boundary of Another World," may now be read in another light, when we see how easily the good man was made the dupe of juggling mediums. Owen "registered in his heart a vow that he would not rest or falter till he had proved this possibility (of spiritual phenomena) to be a probability, or a certainty, or a delusion;" and when, "good, easy man," he had satisfied himself of their reality by attending the bogus spirit *séances* of the Holmeses, he declared it "of all human privileges the greatest to have been permitted to observe these phenomena. To witness them marks an era in one's life."

His account of the "materializations" appeared in the "Atlantic Monthly" almost simultaneously with—in fact, the day before—the fraud perpetrated by the Holmeses was exposed; and Owen telegraphed to Boston to cut it out, but too late—the magazine having been published with a slip disclaiming any editorial responsibility in the matter. When poor Owen found this he broke down, and is said to have cried like a child. His mind—which had doubtless been weakened by the thought that "visions are about"—gave way under this rude shock altogether, and the shattered wreck of this scholar and gentleman was consigned to a lunatic asylum.

I am glad to learn that he is sufficiently recovered to leave now; but surely the spectacle of this poor old man—lingering as he did with those "horrible shadows," those "unreal mockeries" around him—should be a warning light to others sailing on a sea of doubt towards the rocks of Spiritualism!

"IOTA"* is an individual—(he is not only a man but a M.I.C.E.)—and a very terrible fellow indeed. Never a Spiritual *mêlée* but the bold "Iota" is there found, prancing upon his hobby-horse; he rushes into a wordy war with the keenest zest, "trailing" his coat, using a pen for a shillelagh, and gallantly hitting out right and left at the first head he sees, whether friends or foes.

I have been in the wars with this fire-eating engineer: he challenged me for £1,000 to produce such manifestations as enter into the *repertoire* of the mediumistic craft, which I at once accepted, and undertook to rap and raise tables, produce spirit-lights, spirit-faces, and suspend myself in mid-air, under the same conditions as Home; but "Iota" knew better than to part with his money upon such easy terms, and insisted that I should be bound, and held by a committee, and that a light should be struck at any moment during the manifestations. I would like to see the medium who can consent to this! When the media submit to such tests, I may safely promise to do likewise.

SCIENTIFIC INVESTIGATION.

In England science soon failed to find anything in Spiritualism worthy of its attention. Two or three gentle-

---

* Mr. Algernon Joy, Honorary Secretary to the National Association of Spiritualists.

men, with "F.R.S." attached to their names, have busied themselves with the "spirits," and recorded their belief in them; but their ceaseless loquacity has had no effect upon the "masterly inactivity" of scientific men in general.

That "wave" Spiritualists are so fond of talking about, of investigation, has gone over to Russia, where, through the intervention of the Hon. Alexandre Aksakof, Russian Imperial Councillor, and Professor Bontleroff—both related to "airy Daniel" by marriage—the St. Petersburg University resolved to examine into the phenomena. Mediums not being plentiful in the Czar's dominions, the boys Joseph and William Petty, of Newcastle, England, aged respectively thirteen and seventeen years, were taken to the Russian capital, but have returned discomfited, not being able to manifest *even in the dark;* and the reason assigned for the failure is—*the mother of the boys was not with them.* This is a terribly weak ending after the flourish of trumpets we heard when the Spiritualistic world was *en fête* at this recognition by the Russian *savans*.

SERJEANT COX, albeit he dabbles a little in the mystic line himself, being charmed by the glamour of the ghostly idea, has "done the State some service" by pointing out a few of the weaknesses in the Spiritual armour, thus:

"All the prescribed conditions are such as facilitate trickery, if designed, and to prevent, and not to promote inquiry. Friends are posted on either side of the curtain, as if to exclude a too curious eye. If any strangers are present, hands are to be held. The singing usually invited diverts attention, and prevents the intent ear from perceiving movements behind the curtain. The hand of the 'spirit' is not to be held, only opened to a hasty touch. Visitors not known to have the firmest faith are placed in a semicircle, and conditioned not to rush forward or grasp. A considerable time elapses before the form appears. The sitting is not closed and the curtains withdrawn, so that all may see, for a long time after the form has retired. None are admitted behind the curtain until the most perfect confidence is placed in their previously assured faith. Even the few thus favoured were not admitted at once, but by slow degrees—thus far to-night—a little farther another night—as trial proved the extent of their inquisitorial purposes or powers.

"The unquestionable likeness of the form to the medium. When I saw them they were not merely resemblances; they were facsimiles. I had carefully noted the shape of the eyebrows, which cannot be altered, and they were the same in the medium and the form. The hands were identical. The movements of the body were precisely similar. Now, what is the answer to this most suspicious fact? There is no escape from it. Either the form is 'the double' of the medium, or it is another being. If the double of the medium, and the substantial form is borrowed from the medium, the weight of the substantial form must be so much taken from the weight of the medium. If this were so, the medium must be a mere shell, and must die. The theory of 'the double' is therefore exploded. But if Katey and Florence are distinct beings from Miss Cook and Miss Showers—the forms of persons who once lived—to wit, Annie Morgan and Florence Maples—and whose atomic spirit structure is suddenly changed into molecular structure, how comes it that they precisely resemble Miss Cook and Miss Showers? It would be a marvellous coincidence if the real Annie Morgan claimed to have been a facsimile of Miss Cook, and it would be a combination of coincidences almost amounting to impossibility, that Florence Maples should also bear an exact resemblance to Miss Showers.

"But the difficulties do not end there. Assuming the

forms to be Mesdames Morgan and Maples, who lived on earth some years ago, and who ever since have been dwelling in spiritland, how comes it that they think the thoughts, and speak the language, and have the manners of girls of the year 1874, instead of the very different ideas, structure of talk, and manners of their own time? And, more than this, why does Miss Maples play upon the piano tunes that have been composed since her death, and sing songs of recent date, instead of those that were known to her in life? It might have been thought that the best proof the two spirits could have given of their identity would have been to present themselves *as they were* in life, instead of appearing *as the mediums are*."

Mr. WILLIAM CROOKES, F.R.S., Editor of the "Chemical News" and the "Quarterly Journal of Science," is a very awkward gentleman to encounter, and one I should feel some diffidence in criticising, were I not sure that he shows to much greater advantage as the discoverer of the metal *thallium*, than as an "investigator" of "the phenomena called Spiritual."

Mr. Crookes puts forward his "proofs" so ingenuously, with such an air of good faith, that one might be startled if we did not know how easily the gentleman can be hoodwinked. Anyhow, his name, with the three letters behind it, has drawn considerable attention to Spiritualism, and his adherence to the cause has been a prop to the crumbling fabric of the "Pantheon."

When Mr. Crookes came out as an "inquirer," he said, "Hitherto I have seen nothing to convince me of the 'Spiritual' theory. In such an inquiry the intellect demands that the spiritual proof must be absolutely incapable of being cleared away; it must be so strikingly and convincingly true, that we cannot, dare not, deny it. . . . *In a subject which perhaps more than any other lends it-*

self to trickery and deception, the precautions against fraud appear to have been in most cases totally insufficient." And in his "Spiritualism Viewed by the Light of Modern Science," he says: "The explanations given to me, *both orally and in most of the books I have read*, are shrouded in such a ponderosity of style—such an attempt at disguising poverty of ideas in grandiloquent language—that I feel it impossible, after driving off *the frothy diluent*, to discern a crystalline residue of meaning."

But, for all this, Mr. Crookes accepts phenomena upon what *I* consider very easy terms indeed; "Precaution" appears to have been nowhere in the race—"Blind faith" maintaining the lead from start to finish. The "Quarterly Review" (October, 1871) declares that "he entered upon the inquiry with *an avowed foregone conclusion of his own*, based on evidence which he admitted to be scientifically incomplete; and this obviously deprives his convictions of their objective reality, or even that small measure of value to which his scientific character might have given it a claim, if his testimony had been impartial;" and this fact may lead us to read in a new light his "Notes on an Inquiry into the Phenomena called Spiritual."[*]

Mr. Crookes has been a persistent "investigator," and is great at capturing the female media. He says: "As a personal favour, I have more than once been allowed to be present at meetings that presented rather the form of a religious ceremony than of a Spiritualistic *séance*. . . . Only once or twice have I been able to carry off the priestess from her shrine, and in my own house, surrounded by my own friends, to enjoy opportunities of testing the phenomena I had witnessed elsewhere under less conclusive conditions."

---

[*] "Quarterly Journal of Science," January, 1874.

Odds and Ends.

It is a very common thing for Mr. Crookes to see ghosts and converse with them. Miss Cook's " Katey King " was *very human*, and the " scientist " " has taken its pulse, counted its rate of breathing, cut off some of its hair, and by means of powerful artificial light, photographed it at various times, so that forty-four negatives of its portrait, or full length figures, have been obtained."*

As a believer Mr. Crookes is all very well; as an investigator he is a failure. His accordion test with Mr. Home was absurd: fancy a scientific man putting an accordion in a cage *under the table*, and then letting the medium use one hand to play upon it! Why, in the name of common sense, have it *underneath* the table? This is one of those things which a noble lord—much given to the " Haymarket "—would say " no fellah can understand ! "†
In " Miss " Fay's case his investigation failed to discover the simple tricks of her dark *séance*, which many a schoolboy would see through; and his partizanship, both in the case of this lady and Miss Cook, deprives his statements of the least value save with the prejudiced few to whom, I suppose, they are directed.

How strange that Mr. Crookes should write in his first paper (July, 1870), " I confess that the reasoning of some Spiritualists would almost seem to justify Faraday's severe statement—that many dogs have the power of coming to more logical conclusions " ! Since then Mr. Crookes has come to be at one with these illogical people—these cloudy philosophers—and has gaily played upon the Spiritualistic pipe. England has not danced yet, but there may be " a good time coming," so " wait a little longer," Mr. Crookes.

---

* " The Nonconformist," September 15th, 1875.

† Mr. Sothern, himself a reputed medium in America, but who has declared his belief that " every spiritual exhibitor who makes money by the exhibition is a swindler."

The F.R.S. is very hard upon the conjurors, and I will give him *my* views of their merits relatively to those of the mediums. Medium and conjuror means the same thing, only the former is a very poor stick, indeed, at his trade : a bad conjuror will make a good medium any day. The mediumistic conjurors devote themselves to "spirit phenomena," and as it is their specialty, they should be unapproachable in it. But, see ! the spirit juggler shall keep you singing hymns for two hours in a darkened room (his own room, too !) and then pronounce the circumstances unfavourable. Could the ordinary professor of legerdemain, could the illusionist, be allowed such latitude? No ! The latter *must* produce the effects whether the audience be "sympathetic" (*i.e.*, gullible) or not. My audience is only sympathetic so long as I succeed in amusing or interesting it; waiting in the dark for two hours—effects *nil*—would scarcely be endured !

THE DIALECTICAL SOCIETY—a debating club founded in 1867, under the presidency of Sir John Lubbock, Bart.—may be said to have given a lift to Spiritualism, which, in its turn, says the "Spiritualist," "raised the little society into public notice."

A committee of its members undertook to "inquire into the nature and reality of the phenomena commonly called Spiritual," and divided itself into six sub-committees for that purpose. These, in 1871, presented a voluminous report on their own responsibility—the society, through its secretary, Mr. Ford, repudiating it. Of this document the "Saturday Review" (October 21st, 1871) says :

"Half the sub-committees saw nothing whatever, and of the remaining three, one only held the so-called communication by means of signals ; and yet the committee calmly states that the reports substantially corroborate each other, and that 'a large majority of the committee have become actually witnesses to several phases of the phenomena without the aid or presence of any professional medium!' What is meant by 'substantial corroborations' we must leave to be decided by persons who call themselves a 'Dialectical Society.' We could not, under the circumstances, very well imagine less corroboration, as we understand the term.

"We will next endeavour to form some estimate of the acuteness of the sub-committee which was more favoured than its neighbours. The most remarkable narrative which it records, and which we have no space to give at length, depends for its point chiefly upon the following circumstance: A spirit revealed to the party that his executor had embezzled certain money which the spirit had left to one of the ladies present. Now, as it is said, neither the lady nor any other person had been previously aware of this fact; and, so far from suspecting the executor, she had made him a handsome present for his kind discharge of his duty. On investigation, however, it turned out that the spirit was correct in his statements, and the committee wondered greatly at the unaccountable revelation thus made.

"It is a very pretty story, but two remarks must be added. In the first place, the investigation above mentioned consisted in the lady's husband referring to certain 'letters' which were in his wife's possession, and which had not been looked at for years. It is clear, then, that she had looked at them, and that she might have ascertained the facts for herself. The question is whether we are to believe that a spirit gave her the information some years afterwards through a table, or whether she had some dim recollection of the facts, and unconsciously directed the utterances of the table by a process too familiar to need explanation. There is yet a third hypothesis, which, as uncomplimentary to the lady's sincerity, we decline to state explicitly; but it certainly seems more probable than the interference of a spirit. In fact, the wonder disappears as soon as we see that the information was easily accessible without a trace of supernatural means. But, in the next place, Dr. Edmonds tells us in a very sensible letter that the report of this incident as first composed was substantially different, and that, on his pointing out an 'internal incoherence or contradiction,' it was re-written. The writer of the report tries to put a different colour upon this incident; but when the evidence as to the most wonderful story related is thus confused and uncertain, we hope that we are not very sceptical in treating the whole affair as too absurd to deserve further notice."

"Punch" (Dec. 1869) had a fine rub for the "Dialecticals" upon the appearance of the following advertisement in the papers:

"*To Proprietors of Haunted Houses.*—A few gentlemen wish to have the opportunity of visiting a house said to be haunted, situate in or near London, for the purpose of scientific investigation." The great comic periodical advertised the matter thus:

"WANTED A GHOST.

"Wanted a ghost of whatever variety,
Fitted to mingle in learned society;
Able to work on the feelings electric
Of *savans* devoted to themes dialectic.

"Wanted a house full of wondrous hoards,
Bells autophonic and creakiest boards;
Regions by restless departed ones haunted,
That's what to keep up the spirits is wanted.

"Wanted to sit up the whole of the night,
Waiting the advent of goblin or sprite;

Wanted from t'other side of Jordan to roam,
Vampires inclined for a go-in at home.

"Wanted some dæmon to give us a note
What it is keeps airy DANIEL afloat!
Wanted at least elementary traces
What is the power that elongates his braces.

"Wanted to know what on earth are the merits
That make Mrs. Marshall affected by 'sperrits.'
Wanted to know why respectable dead
Come back to life at five shillings a head.

"Wanted old ladies and children to fright,
Waked up by cats in the dead of the night;
Wanted this age of inquiry to daunt—
That's what these pseudo-philosophers want.

"Wanted to galvanize once and again
All the exploded old tricks of Cock Lane!
Wanted to make a white sheet and a post
Go down once more as a genuine ghost.

"Wanted—how idle such needs 't is to flaunt!
Blessed if I think they know what 't is they want.
Wanted—it seems to me, don't it to you?—
Dialecticians want something to do!"

CHAPTER XIV.

"THE PANTHEON OF PROGRESS."

I HAVE now given a sketch of some prominent points in the past and present history of Spiritualism, and we may pause to look back upon its course, and see if its work, during a life of thirty years, is such as to justify the high-sounding title heading this chapter, which it has "annexed."

I have shown the tricks of the "sweet mejums" (as Artemus Ward has it) and the hocus-pocus of their profession. From the very first there has been, to put it in the mildest form, a suspicion of fraud. Davis's high-falutin was rather due to his own quick wit, and the inspiration of his "coaches," than any influence of the spirits; indeed, Levingston, who should know something about it, accused him of being a tool in the hands of Messrs. Lyon and Fishbough. Then the "physical manifestations" of the Foxes may or may not hold such near relationship as I believe they do to the Cock Lane ghost; but even if not, their rapping and their table-moving can both be accounted for without trenching upon the supernatural. Home was contradicted point-blank upon several important points by Sir David Brewster, and generally failed to produce any extraordinary "manifestations"—nothing more than rapping and table-moving—save in the presence of the faithful. Several of the most remarkable stories (for we have to take everything on hearsay) are tinged with such a partizanship, and so confused withal, that any unprejudiced mind must entertain very grave doubts of their veracity, though not necessarily impugning the good faith of the writers. Then the Davenports, though some of the Spiritualists still cling to their mediumship, are generally discredited; and I think Mr. Cooke and myself have shown sufficient to convince the public, at any rate, that the supposed "spirit power" of the "juggling Gemini" was and is (for they are still at their old games on the Continent) a terrible swindle.

Perhaps I should recapitulate how Foster's and Colchester's tricks are stale even with the "wizards" who amuse without defrauding the public, though they are still to be found rejuvenated by the media, like old rams dressed up lamb fashion. Must I also remind you once again of the many more than suspicious "materializations" about which even some "weak-kneed" Spiritualists are doubtful; of the frauds, patent to all, of the Holmeses, the Spirit Photographers, &c. ? Shall I mention the "Trance Media," and the "Inspirationists," who never possess higher powers than are to be found in those who are popularly said to be "gifted with the gab," and who usually speak "an infinite deal of nothing"? And must I note the supicious fact that while you may wait an hour for any other form of spirit manifestation, *and then not get it*, the "Inspirationist" has *always* got her, or his, "spirit guides" well in hand, and can dash off into any subject in the wordiest and most ornate of canters at a moment's notice? Even supposing a few of the media to believe honestly in their power, and I am not illiberal enough to say this may not be the case, this fact should not be enough to convince a reasonable man or woman of the truth of what they say, though I know the weight earnestness and conviction always carry with them. Can any of these people through their spirit guides solve the problem of the icy North, or fix the source of the Nile, that African mystery to the heart of which Stanley so gallantly struggles now? I wot not! But until they do this—or something like it—and give us more than tall talk and stale juggling tricks, palmed off upon too credulous believers as the communications and the work of the ethereal hosts, the world will still be "sceptical."

What a libel upon "the spirits of the just made perfect," that through some possibly debased and drunken "medium" they shall give ignorant or frivolous messages to mankind! But so it is, according to the Spiritual theory. Examine the communications from the spirits, and out of the stupid mass see if you can get one grain of wisdom higher than the standard of the medium's mind it emanates from, or, as they say, comes through; see if one of the class so industriously working the "gold mine"—from "'Dan' to Beersheba"—can give you a single "tip" of any higher value than a sporting prophet's, which *may* come right, but is far more likely to prove wrong.

But the media, who should like Cæsar's wife be above suspicion, have too often been caught tripping for ordinary onlookers to place any reliance on them, though they still remain dear to the faithful few, who take the prodigal ones back again and condone their past offences with new faith. But recent events in Paris "have cast a temporary shadow" over the cause; the Holmes's *fiasco* is not yet out of men's minds; and Liverpool has been a terrible rock ahead, lately. Mediumship does not pay so well as of yore, even the hoodwinked "faithful" being chary of giving credence to all the "physical manifestations" and "materializations" that are about. Then again the market is overstocked; and *the conjurors perform the tricks so much better!*

So at the end of thirty years the managers of this Spiritual business, on taking stock, may cogitate thus: When we deduct from the "phenomena" all that may be trickery, or due to an "exalted"—and, so far, an unnatural and diseased—state of the brain; or to natural causes, whether labelled "Unconscious Cerebration" or "Psychic Force" (the existence of which we doubt!), we shall have few "miracles" on hand. And then, we fear, our custom is falling off! Time was when fanatic faith and long purses were at our service (and both were drawn upon pretty largely!); but now, what with waning faith and bankrupt treasury, the "Pantheon" is like to come about our ears, unless we shore it up with that very unsafe beam—Reincarnation! We have certainly some good servants left, and Varley, Crookes, and Co. are active agents; but our literary men, though amiable, are weak, and we are not written up properly; indeed, our trade organs, the "Spiritualist" and the "Medium," are in a state of inanition. The race of earnest workers is dying out, and the few converts made are of a low order,* the middle class being fenced about by a heartless scepticism. The English press is still unconverted, and point to the fact that many we look upon as customers examine our wares from motives of curiosity only,† some "for the fun of the thing," the *blasé*, and a few who think "there's something in it," but who cannot make up their minds to buy. Such is the out-

---

* With the colliers in the extreme north of England, the Spiritual goods "go like wildfire."—" Medium."

† For simply attending a *séance*, a son of the late Charles Dickens was hailed as a convert, "than which no statement could be more untrue," wrote the gifted novelist.—"All the Year Round," July 28th, 1860.

look, and an unpleasant one for the "Pantheon," which seems to "progress" backwards!

Now, in conclusion, I fearlessly ask for an honest verdict, whether it can be a good thing for any nineteenth-century Englishman to be running after a "Religion" which teaches nothing, and unsettles faith in all the Churches; and a system of morality which is capable of being distorted, and has, in some instances at least, *led up to* (for I will not blame Spiritualism with all the evil) such unsavoury doctrines as "Spiritual Marriages," and "Free Love," against which Artemus Ward "pored 4th his indignashun!"

I have purposely given the various opinions of "unbelievers," and quoted somewhat largely from Spiritualistic sources; while I have "nothing extenuated" I have certainly "set down nought in malice," being as willing to allow the abilities and many virtues of some of the followers of Spiritualism as I am eager to expose the poverty-stricken tricks of the professed media, which, instead of investigation at the hands of the Royal Society, rather demand the attention of the authorities of Scotland Yard, as being a means of obtaining money under false pretences. If such a happy investigation *should* come, what a chance for the Holmeses, *et hoc genus omnes*, to demand the intervention of the spirits! If they got free from the bonds of the Metropolitan Police we might have greater faith in the power of the mediums than we have in—

"THE PANTHEON OF PROGRESS!"

www.ingramcontent.com/pod-product-compliance
Lightning Source LLC
Chambersburg PA
CBHW020243170426
43202CB00008B/198